# START-UP
# OR START OVER.
# JUST START.

*Written by*
*Dr. Jillian Zambon and 12 Inspiring Authors*

ISBN:979-8-9882308-1-6 (Paperback)

ISBN: 979-8-9882308-0-9 (Digital Online Version)

# Contents

Introduction.. .. .. .. .. .. .. .. .. .. .. .. .. .. .. .. .. .. .. .. .. ..4

**Failure to Footing**
BY DR. JILL ZAMBON. .. .. .. .. .. .. .. .. .. .. .. .. .. .. .. .. 5

**I'm Too Pretty For Jail**
BY JAIME NICOLE .. .. .. .. .. .. .. .. .. .. .. .. .. .. .. .. .. ..13

**Thriving on a healthy "NO."**
BY INES KAPS.. .. .. .. .. .. .. .. .. .. .. .. .. .. .. .. .. .. ..20

**Finding Your Inner Butterfly**
BY KATIE JORDAN .. .. .. .. .. .. .. .. .. .. .. .. .. .. .. ..29

**Turn Your Pain into Power**
BY SUMMER MONTABONE .. .. .. .. .. .. .. .. .. .. .. .. ..37

**The Power of Persistence: Overcoming the
Hurdles of Entrepreneurship**
BY JOCELYN GALICIA POWELL .. .. .. .. .. .. .. .. ..47

**Breaking Free and Starting Over: A Journey to
Emotional Mastery**
BY RASHDA SHANAZ. .. .. .. .. .. .. .. .. .. .. .. .. .. .. ..55

**Arriving Right on Time**
BY LEANN LAZAR .. .. .. .. .. .. .. .. .. .. .. .. .. .. .. ..64

**Not Your Average Passive**
BY SARAH MILLER .. .. .. .. .. .. .. .. .. .. .. .. .. .. .. ..71

**True Success Comes From Genuine Passion and Drive**
BY M.H. TA, DDS. .. .. .. .. .. .. .. .. .. .. .. .. .. .. .. .. ..80

**Rising from the Ashes: Creating a New Life After Burnout**
BY DR. KRISTEN C. ECCLESTON THE
NEURODIVERSE TEACHER ™ .. .. .. .. .. .. .. .. .. .. ..88

**Getting Out of My Own Way**
BY ADRIENNE KENNIE.. .. .. .. .. .. .. .. .. .. .. .. .. ..97

**Writing Your Story: The Educator to Entrepreneur Journey**
BY MEAGAN BEAM.. .. .. .. .. .. .. .. .. .. .. .. .. .. .. ..105

# Introduction

Starting and growing a business is no easy feat, especially for women. According to a report by American Express, in 2020, women-owned businesses accounted for 42% of all businesses in the United States, yet only 4.3% of those businesses generated over a million dollars in revenue. This staggering statistic showcases the difficulties women face when it comes to entrepreneurship.

But despite these challenges, women entrepreneurs are on the rise. They are defying the odds and making their mark in the business world. In this book, 14 women entrepreneurs share their stories about starting a business, re-starting a business, starting their business over, or growing their business.

These women come from various backgrounds and industries, but they all share a common thread: the passion and determination to succeed. They have faced obstacles such as limited resources, lack of support, and societal expectations, but they have persevered and succeeded.

Through their stories, readers will gain valuable insights into the world of entrepreneurship. They will learn about the struggles, triumphs, and lessons learned from these women who have taken the leap into entrepreneurship.

This book is not just for aspiring women entrepreneurs, but for anyone who wants to learn from successful business leaders. These women are trailblazers who have shattered the glass ceiling and paved the way for future generations of women entrepreneurs.

Their stories are powerful and inspiring, and we hope they will encourage and motivate readers to pursue their own dreams and passions, no matter how difficult the journey may seem.

# Failure to Footing

## By Dr. Jill Zambon

D r. Jillian Zambon is an accomplished education and business professional with over 15 years of experience in the field. She holds an Ed.D. in Healthcare Administration, an MBA in Project Management, and a PMP certification. Jillian has worked in various roles throughout her career, including as a director, product manager, and project manager. Jillian has a passion for leadership and has demonstrated her skills in leading teams and implementing successful projects. She has a proven track record of improving operational efficiency, developing and implementing strategies, and building high-performing teams. Throughout her career, Jillian has been recognized for her exceptional leadership and management skills and has received numerous awards and honors for her contributions to education and business. She is also an active member of various professional organizations and is dedicated to giving back to her community. Jillian is a lifelong learner and believes in continuous improvement. She enjoys mentoring others and sharing her knowledge and experience with aspiring professionals.

**Connect with Dr. Jill:**

Facebook: https://www.facebook.com/jillian.zambon/

Instagram: https://www.instagram.com/jillzambon/

LinkedIn: https://www.linkedin.com/in/jillian-zambon-ed-d-mba-pmp-a5959725/

Website: https://zambonjill.wixsite.com/start-up-or-start-ov

# Failure to Footing
## By Dr. Jill Zambon

I was one of those women who looked down on the stay-at-home mom. I looked down on women who would give up their entire careers for their children. It would be silly to throw away years of education and career growth to raise *a kid.*

That was until I became a mom in 2013. I didn't immediately have the desire to quit my job and stay at home with my daughter all day. I had just taken a new job and had zero maternity leave unless I wanted to go on unpaid leave. I couldn't afford to do that at the time. Luckily, I had an excellent (male) boss at the time, who allowed me to "work" from home for months and ease back into going to the office full time.

It took me a long time, and a global pandemic, to realize that work was taking priority over my daughter. It took nine years, to be exact. When the COVID pandemic hit, it was a perfect storm of events. My daughter's father had just moved away. That meant Jayde was with me 100% of the time rather than going with him every other weekend. I was working a lot because my employer was responsible for all the pre-clinical trials for the COVID vaccine. Winter was around the corner, which meant snow removal, house heating, freezing pipes, freezing temps, and all the other harsh parts of New England winter. I made a weak attempt at homeschooling, but the day usually ended up being a movie marathon for Jayde while I sat on conference calls for nine hours daily. It made sense at the time because if I missed a work call, the world was doomed!

I couldn't understand why I was struggling so badly. I didn't have to stay there anymore. I didn't have to work to care for a home in

New England. I didn't have to stay in that school district because they weren't going to school. I began searching for places where kids were in school.

I always wanted to live near the beach, and now seemed like the time to make it happen. I started to Google "best places to live in Florida as a single parent" and found an area with a good school system, pretty quiet, and commutable distance to Tampa, Florida. In two weeks, I had the house on the market, our stuff listed on Facebook Marketplace, and a yard sale planned. I sold almost everything we owned, packed up, and drove me, my daughter, and our dog 23 hours in a car from New Hampshire to Florida.

It was a disaster. Problems started before leaving the house. When the moving truck showed up, the DOT tag was duct taped to the side of the box trailer, which had metal sheets dangling off it. The movers started adding "extra charges" to the freight fees, and the next thing I knew, they asked me for another $1,000, or I couldn't get our belongings back.

When we arrived in Florida, the apartment building we were supposed to move into wasn't ready. It was still under construction, so you couldn't walk the property without wearing a hard hat, and they didn't even have their vacancy certificate yet. The apartments didn't have appliances yet, and the model was not ready to be viewed.

Luckily, I found another apartment building with some openings, and we managed to sneak in. Our belongings were still in Connecticut, so we bought twin-sized mattresses and slept on the floor for weeks. In the meantime, we ended up in an entirely different school because we didn't get the planned apartment. Due to your address change, the school I had started enrolling my daughter in differed from where she'd be going. It was COVID, so I wasn't allowed to meet her teachers or administrators in the school. I had to drop her off at a new school to people I had never met and then walk away.

I began to think I had made a HUGE mistake moving to Florida. After a few months in Florida, things started to shift for us. Our belongings finally arrived (with an upcharge because the movers had to walk upstairs). And being in the hustle culture of Florida, I decided to start my own business.

A fashion eCommerce business with sustainable women's clothing was where I landed. Why? Because although I'm a veteran, I'm secretly a hippy who wants to save the earth. I've always been a fashion connoisseur, and, at the time, it felt right. My doctorate was in healthcare, and I have worked in IT for about 12 years. I had zero clue how to start a fashion e-commerce brand. But I just started.

I started watching YouTube videos on fashion design while I ran on the treadmill each morning. I started learning about the manufacturing and design process, how to identify trends, different types of fabrics, etc. But my excitement at the time prevented the logical part of my brain from realizing that during the COVID pandemic, I might be unable to source and manufacture clothing as quickly as I needed.

Finding a manufacturing partner and a supplier was an absolute nightmare. When I finally found a manufacturing partner, their first and second sets of prototypes needed to be up to the desired quality. The fabrics were different from what I had asked for. The colors needed to be corrected—the measurements required to be updated. Everything was just wrong.

At this point, I had sunk enough of my money, time, and energy into the project that I didn't want to give up. But I realized if I wanted to start making money soon (and be able to quit my day job!), then I needed to take a different path.

I decided to start wholesaling sustainable clothing. Wholesale is when the business buys clothing in bulk at a discounted rate, then turns around and marks it up to sell to the customer. So I decided to start wholesaling sustainable apparel. I ordered tees, tanks, and tee shirt dresses made of organic cotton and bamboo and threw them up on a website. I put them up for sale and started to make some sales. Then I expanded the collection. I added rayon dresses (made from eucalyptus trees) and more bamboo and organic cotton items. I added wool products. Anything that was considered a sustainable product and sourced from a female- or minority-owned business, I added it to the website.

But sales stopped. And I couldn't figure out how to make more sales. I tried pop-up trade shows and ads. I even won a TV ad through the SBA and still got no sales. I spent every waking hour outside work making content for this business and trying to sell the products– nothing was happening. I was hitting a wall in my business.

Eventually, I left the business with $85,000 in debt.

But, now I had flipped the internal entrepreneurial switch to ON, and there was no turning back. I attended a Christian conference for entrepreneurs, and two of the wealth-building topics they discussed were real estate and stock trading. These things were foreign, but I wanted to dive in and learn.

That day, I signed up for follow-on workshops in both areas. After attending the real estate conference, I knew I wanted to do more of it. I was in the third home I had purchased using a VA loan, and I had flipped the first two for $11,000 and $27,000 profit, respectively. I realized I had a natural clue about this and decided to jump in. Or at least I tried to.

After close to a year of putting in offers, losing money towards inspections, and trying to use "other people's money" (OPM), I questioned whether real estate investing was a good path for me. In theory, it sounded great. Passive income, building equity over time, using OPM, so I didn't have to use my own money– but finding these deals was like finding a diamond in a haystack. And I was getting discouraged.

So I still faced an issue–I needed to make money now. I had left my corporate job and now felt the impending doom of trying to support a household. I had met a mentor through a speaking program I joined, who said, "Jill. You have been so successful as a single mom. Why don't you help other single moms do the same?" I thought, yeah, that sounds great, but how will I monetize it!?

I had always wanted to write a book, and I knew it would help build my credibility and help me stand apart from the rest– so I decided to start there. When I spoke with the publisher, they said, "Why don't you include other women in the book? That way, you don't have to carry the whole burden, and they can help offset all the costs of publishing, editing, cover design, marketing, and all the other costs you would have to pay for out of pocket alone?" I thought, what a great idea!

So I set out to recruit single moms like me, who wanted to share their stories and empower the world. We wrote our first book, *Shattering the Stigma of Single Motherhood.* I quickly realized that although my heart was with single moms, I felt I had a more significant calling. I decided to open my book publishing opportunities to all women in business and recruited a highly diverse group of female entrepreneurs. Again, I felt like I still wasn't quite in alignment.

As I write this chapter, I am again at a pivot in my business. While attending church one weekend, I felt I should look into ministry and get a theology and ministry degree. Self-doubt crept in, and I thought, "Who are *you* to get into ministry? You have made SO many mistakes in life." I tucked the idea into the back of my mind, thinking that was the end of it. But, the following weekend at church, a woman about my age stood up on the stage explaining that she was going to school for ministry and although she had three kids and a full-time job, she was able to manage. I wondered if this was a Higher Power telling me to pursue it further, so I went up and talked to the woman after the service. Things quickly progressed, and the next thing I knew, I was meeting with one of the pastors at the church and then the Chief Academic Officer at the college. I've contacted local churches to partner with them to build Christian-based conferences. While I still pursue other opportunities (such as business and real estate investing), I am seriously exploring the path of ministry.

I can tell you from my experience with one failed business and one that was profitable but wasn't quite in alignment with who I am, and I am here to say– keep going until you find something that makes you happy. There is something that is BOTH profitable AND can make you happy. You do not have to choose between those two things. Here are some of the key things I wish I had considered when I first started my business:

1. Just start. There's no good time. There are no perfect conditions. You're never going to know everything. Starting a business feels like a trust fall, where you don't even know if someone is behind you to catch you. You are just jumping off the cliff and

grabbing for some wings as you go. It can be done. It has been done. And I believe that if you have found something you're passionate enough about, you can make it happen.

2. Don't be afraid to pivot. Someone once sent me a nasty text about "whatever my business idea of the week would be." Well, guess what? Sometimes you have to change directions. If what you're doing isn't making you happy or making you money, it's time to pivot.

3. Go your own way. Some influencers will tell you to hustle 24x7x365. Others will ask you to work as minimally as possible. Do whatever works for you. I'm a single mom, so my max number of hours to work daily is generally 6 hours. I'll sometimes do nightly calls, maybe once or twice a week. I've stopped, for the most part, working on weekends. Running yourself ragged will not help you create a profitable and stable business.

4. Stick to your ethics. Business often falls in a gray area. Decisions are not always a clear-cut black-or-white choice. It'll be somewhere in the middle, and it's up to you to decide if you align with it or not. Just because someone else is doing it doesn't mean you have to.

5. Have fun. Starting a business is hard. You may struggle financially. You don't know where your path ends, so you're always taking the next right step and then course-correcting if that step doesn't work. If you make the process fun, you will make it more enjoyable. Have fun.

If you have found any inspiration in this story, find me on Facebook: https://www.facebook.com/jillian.zambon/, Instagram: https://www.instagram.com/jillzambon/, and LinkedIn: https://www.linkedin.com/in/jillian-zambon-ed-d-mba-pmp-a5959725/

# I'm Too Pretty For Jail

## By Jaime Nicole

aime Nicole is a beauty consultant, a licensed cosmetologist and owner of the award-winning Jaime Nicole Salon. In her three-decade career as a hair and makeup expert, she has built a six-figure business, glamorized thousands of clients and honed her expertise with additional training from Vidal Sassoon, Aveda, Great Lengths USA, Eufora International and more. When she's not working in her San Diego salon, you can find her training and coaching the next generation of stylists who seek her out for mentorship.

In an effort to help her clients look and feel good on the inside and out, she recently launched her Jaime Nicole Beauty Collagen. After struggling with joint pain in her hands and hearing her customers' desire to grow stronger hair and nails, she developed the pure and scientifically-proven formula along with industry experts.

Jaime Nicole lives in San Diego, California, with her husband, two children, and two English Bulldogs.

**Contact Jaime:**

LinkedIn: https://www.linkedin.com/in/jaime-nicole-berkes-castillo-bb7b171/

Facebook: https://www.facebook.com/jaime.berkes

Instagram: @jnbeautycollagen

Website: https://jaimenicolebeautycollagen.com/

# I'm Too Pretty For Jail
## By Jaime Nicole

I had just turned 25 years old. I was single, nine months pregnant, and working 60 hours a week doing hair. I'll never forget it. It was Friday, August 22nd, 2003. I was at the salon shampooing a client's hair and my water broke. Thank God I was wearing black pants, and nobody could tell.

When I was done shampooing my client's hair, I told the owner of the salon that my water broke and I needed to go to the hospital once I finished my client's haircut. I told the owner he needed to reschedule the rest of my night. The owner was so shocked that I was still working, that he told all the other stylists. They all stared at me in disbelief. As soon as I finished the haircut and blow-dry, I drove to my house, grabbed the hospital bag that I had pre-packed, and drove myself to the hospital on a Friday night in San Diego, California traffic.

My beautiful healthy son was born at 10:00 p.m. that night. I was up and ready to go home after I gave birth, but the doctor made me stay until Monday. On Tuesday, four days after giving birth to my son, I was back at the salon working. Unfortunately, I didn't qualify for disability or get any paid time off, so I had to do what a single Mom does best. Work my butt off to provide for my baby!

I continued to work 12-18 hour days doing hair during the day (rushing home to see my baby on any break I got) and selling skin care for a company at night. I made it to Regional Vice President in the company and received a company-paid Mercedes Benz. My son would go to meetings with me. I remember him being two years old and people would ask him who the President of the company was and he would tell them. We did this for two years and boy was I really feeling the pinch of working for other people's dreams. So, I saved all that money and opened my own salon.

I've owned my salon in California for 17 years and despite the 2008 recession and the 2020 pandemic, sales continued to increase. For me, the third year in business was the hardest.

By year three, I had expanded and opened a spa next door to the salon. I was 27 when I opened my salon, and I knew nothing about Workman's Compensation insurance. No salon I had ever worked at had it.

One day a representative from the labor board walked into my salon and asked me for my Workmen's Compensation insurance policy. I had 15 employees present at the time. I got fined $1000 for each employee so $15,000 and was looking at three years jail time. I hired a business attorney and had to go to two different court hearings one for civil court and one for criminal court.

The civil court hearing was first. I lost and had to pay the fine. The criminal court hearing was two months later and because I lost a civil case, I knew I was going to lose the criminal case. This was the most stressful two months of my life. I was a single mom, and I didn't know what I was going to do with my son if I went to jail for three years.

Now you may be wondering, what happened to the father? I didn't even get into the abuse or infidelity I put up with my son's father or all of the thousands of dollars I had to spend in court for custody. But regardless of the circumstances, he and I are still friends and he has always been in my son's life. And let me tell you why. If I can give you one piece of advice, this would be my advice to you. Coming from a child with divorced parents, a very messy divorce. My parents never got along. My brother, my sister, and I were always on pins and needles. Every time they were going to be around each other at a holiday, special occasion, or event for one of us, or one of their grandchildren. I believe this is what caused the stomach issues I've had in my entire life from all of the stress. My mom held onto hate and bitterness for years and has had cancer three times. Life is short and I wasn't going to put my son through what my parents put us through so forgive, you don't have to forget, but truly forgive your ex so that you can move on with your life and be happy and give your children the best life they deserve.

At the criminal hearing, instead of three years, of jail time, I was given three years probation. Fast forward to seven years after the trial, and after a lot of hard work, I met my husband. A year later we had our daughter. My husband was in the army for the first 10 years of our marriage, so it still felt like I was a single mom, even though I was married. My husband is now retired from the military. I finally feel like I am not doing this parenting thing alone. My son is doing great. He is in college now and attends UCSD. He is an aspiring anesthesiologist. Quite the opposite of my daughter who does Jiu-jitsu and plays basketball.

Despite overcoming multiple hardships in my career and business, one thing, I didn't predict was how difficult being a hairstylist would be on my body. As the owner of an award-winning, six-figure hair salon, with almost three decades of experience, my body started to wreak havoc. By the end of the workday, my hands would cramp so badly that I couldn't open a jar of sauce to make dinner. I also suffered from tennis elbow from blow-drying hair all day long. I started to desperately search for a solution to a problem that could have ended my career.

That is when I found collagen. I turned to different Collagens for my pain and none of them were working. I called my brother who is in the health and supplement industry and asked him why. He had me send him the labels and he explained to me that the ingredients were all harmful to my health. They were filled with chemicals, preservatives, and fillers. So I, along with industry experts, created my own pure trademarked collagen that took my pain away in the first week. This was all during Covid when my industry was hit very hard and my salon business was shut down for months. Being able to pivot in your career or business during tough times is crucial for success. Jaime Nicole Beauty Collagen was launched on Valentine's Day 2022.

Jaime Nicole Beauty Collagen is a collagen powder you put in your daily drink for Hair, Skin, Nails, Joint Health, and Bone Health.

It's unflavored so it doesn't change the taste of whatever you put it in and the trademarked collagens have all had multi-million dollar clinical studies done on them proven to work and scientifically backed.

Collagen is the most abundant protein in the human body, making up approximately 30% of all your protein by mass. It makes up your hair, teeth, skin, nails, organs, arteries, cartilage, bones, tendons, and ligaments. In fact, 70% of the protein in your skin is made up of collagen. Collagen is what gives skin, its firmness, elasticity, and strength. Wrinkles, sagging skin, and skin spots are all indicators of poor collagen health. Besides skin appearance, poor collagen health is hard to recognize because it's happening inside your body. This is why so many people don't recognize the importance of collagen. Collagen is very important for anti-aging. The loss of collagen can start a full decade prior to the loss of muscle. Starting at the age of 20, you lose just under 10% of your skin's collagen content every decade. So it is important to support collagen health through diet, exercise, and supplements.

Why does a loss of collagen with age matter? Do you have knee pain? Collagen makes up your cartilage, which is what protects your joints by preventing bone from rubbing against bone. In other words, joint pain and osteoarthritis can be caused by a deficiency in collagen.

The amino acid, glycine, which makes up every third amino acid in collagen, is a rate-limiting factor in the formation of our body's most potent endogenous antioxidant called glutathione. Thus, any inflammatory condition can be worsened, or potentially caused by, a deficiency in glycine, which is found in collagen.

Have you noticed that your skin has more wrinkles, and brown spots, or has lost its elasticity and youthfulness? Do you have burns and wounds that don't heal? That could be a collagen deficiency.

Do you have osteoporosis? It turns out that half. Your bone is made of protein with most of that protein being composed of collagen. In other words, a deficiency in collagen can lead to weaker bones.

Are you starting to get the picture of why collagen is so important for health? Since collagen also helps make up your organs (kidney, liver, and heart for example), tendons, ligaments, arteries, vertebrae, etc., almost any condition can be worsened or caused by a deficiency in collagen. In fact, the dramatic rise in diseases such as osteoporosis, tendon ruptures, degenerative disks, and osteoarthritis is thought to be due to, or contributed by, collagen deficiency.

As you can see, collagen has an important role in aging as well as overall health. Countless studies have shown that supplementing with collagen has numerous health benefits. Additionally, Jaime Nicole Beauty Collagen works relatively fast and without any real side effects. I wish you all the best on your journey to obtaining optimal collagen health.

For more information and clinical studies please visit

www.jaimenicolebeautycollagen.com

# Thriving on a healthy "NO."

## By Ines Kaps

I nes Kaps is the founder of WomenLoveConsulting. It's an accelerator program for consulting firms to increase the number of women at all levels.

Ines has created a 6-month down-to-earth coaching program based on her 22 years of consulting experience. It gets results and fits into the daily life of any consultant.

Ines currently sits on the investment board of a global fund. She is a highly regarded program manager on an international level. She has been a team leader in both boutique consulting firms, at KPMG, and has been the head of her own firm in Switzerland. In the pharmaceutical and engineering industries, she is known for delivering global, multi-million-dollar digital transformation projects. Ines is a serial entrepreneur, start-up, and career coach.

She enjoys giving keynote speeches around the world to share her experiences. Ines is married to the best husband in the world. When she is not working, she loves to explore new places with her running shoes.

**Contact Ines:**

LinkedIn: https://www.linkedin.com/in/ineskaps/

Facebook: https://www.facebook.com/ines.kaps/

Instagram: @ineskaps.wlc

Website: www.ineskaps.com

# Thriving on a healthy "NO."
## By Ines Kaps

I felt shattered as my life fell apart. I wanted to go to an engineering high school. I was good at math and physics and wanted to study engineering to learn to work on machines. I knew there were no girls in the school, or maybe just a few. But I didn't care. I already knew several guys who were friends from church. I knew I would l be fine. I would get a high school degree, and although it would take an extra year, I would graduate with a background in engineering. I knew I didn't want to be a lawyer or a doctor, but I loved the idea of being an engineer. My parents wanted me to stay in the public high school in Austria, with the broadest education, so I would have all options to study when I was 18. They didn't want me to specialize at 14.

I remember sitting on my bed in my little room. I looked out the window into the woods. The light was getting darker as it was late afternoon. I was disappointed, angry, and sad. I was the daughter of two high school teachers. At the time, my favorite hobbies were dancing, ballet, and playing the flute. I was a good student and a nice girl. It had not come to my mind to challenge my parent's decision to stay in the public high school. I believed that teachers always knew best. Hence, I accepted their decision and remained at the public high school, including Latin, English, and French as foreign languages.

My life was about good grades, being polite, and being the "teacher's daughter" – the " model of a good student." Then, my parents got divorced when I was 17—just a year before my graduation. My wider family pushed me to be strong – to be strong for my little brother and for my mother.

The perceived responsibility of needing to take care of others didn't change much during my studies in Business Administration or as a young business consultant. I was working hard, and I was friendly to my colleagues and loyal to my customers.

I loved my job as a management consultant. I traveled nationally and internationally and worked with many important and large clients on projects in the engineering and automotive industry. And then, at 27, I was appointed to a big project in France - the largest project of my employer. It was always my dream to work and live in France. Here I was, leading my first 100k project in Nice, France. Being Austrian, I had a structured and detailed approach. We tackle the details and technological issues first, then look at the layout and user interface. In France, you tend to focus on the user interface and then dive into the technical details. In this project, the intense business politics between the IT and the controlling department were challenging to understand – impossible to navigate. My French was good, but not perfect. Everyone was polite and worked with me in English, but the small talk was in French.

I knew something wasn't going right in the project. I couldn't point it out clearly, but I felt uncomfortable as a project manager. My bosses suggested I should keep calm and carry on. They would take care of politics.

The next thing I remember was being shouted at by the client's CFO (Chief Finance Officer). How dare I deliver such incomplete software to him? His data was missing. The reports were awful, and the whole IT was utterly incompetent. I went to the airport in shock and started crying during boarding. The stewardess took me aside and calmed me down. She put me in the empty front row. When we landed, both my parents were there for me. When I returned to the office, it was clear that someone had to help me.

A very experienced program manager and CEO of a strategy consulting firm in his 50s took over the project. We got the project back under control and on track. I later had to apologize to my bosses for ruining the project. When I resigned six months later, the owner of the company said: if I had not left myself, he would have encouraged me to quit. The thought of being asked to resign was painful. Years later, some of my former colleagues said: "We all saw that you were mobbed and managed out." I had not realized it at the time. But I knew I had been right. I had read the signs in this project correctly. All my other projects had been great successes, with customers giving me flowers on the last day of a roll-out.

But this disaster made me strong. And I promised myself to always trust my gut in the future. This situation also strengthened the urge in me to always be treated with respect. I was determined to stop settling for less ever again. Respect became a core value for me.

A few years later, a second pivotal moment occurred while studying for my executive MBA. I worked full-time in a management consulting firm and took a huge loan to finance my MBA. I also saved all my vacations for three years to do the MBA part-time on the weekends.

I was sitting in the final exam preparation session on corporate finance. The tutor was very relaxed and shared his weekend soccer experience and how frustrated he was with all the results. He engaged in a heated discussion on local soccer clubs. I was getting frustrated because the time was running out. After 10 minutes, I raised my hand and asked when he would start on the exam topics. He walked to my desk and started justifying himself. I was getting angry. I did not feel respected as a paying customer and had nothing to lose.

Clearly and directly, I told him that I had paid for this MBA and expected him to deliver on the exam preparation for the final 35 minutes of this session. It was a crystal clear "no – not this way" to him. My heart was racing. My face was red. I was sweating. The class was silent. The tutor stared at me – and then went back to start teaching.

During the break, people congratulated me. My friends sent me encouraging looks. The event was the first time I stood up for myself. I knew I could do it and was proud of myself for setting solid boundaries.

Trusting my gut, knowing my values, and having the confidence to use my voice unleashed my power to lead global multimillion-dollar projects in male-dominated fields successfully. Over time, my superiors assigned me more challenging assignments. A senior director at KPMG explained it with "you are whipping shit into shape" while "de-panicking customers." In senior roles in consulting, challenging clients and complex projects became your daily business.

These large assignments sometimes require managing a difficult person at a client site in an unexpected way. During a Covid lockdown, I led a large software roll-out in a global pharmaceutical company. I was now in my mid-40s. Managing the project globally, from Japan to Germany to the US, was challenging. The cultural differences made it a further complex project. My main task was to manage expectations. For example, when you test a new solution, you expect to find errors – hence the test runs before the roll-out.

The company developing the software had core people leaving, but everyone was working hard. In one debrief meeting with ten people on the Zoom call, a customer team member, Mrs. J, talked herself into a rage because of the errors she had found. I tried to calm her down. I tried to interrupt her. But she was in her zone. The atmosphere was uncomfortable for everyone. So, I had to stop her with a clear "no."My only chance was to put her on mute. At this moment, I started sweating, and my heart was racing. So, I put her on mute. I took a deep breath. And now, I could explain the situation and allow the other team members to share their experiences.

Interestingly, Mrs. J unmuted herself after a few moments and returned calmly. After the meeting, the manager on the client's side called me. She said that she was impressed with how I had handled the situation. I had never muted a customer before. My action did not harm my working relationship with the "muted woman Mrs. J." We talked about it a few days later in a 1:1, and she apologized.

My key learnings from this experience are

✦  I had perceived my actions as harsher than the people around me.

✦  As a leader, I must go into a conflict to protect the team.

✦  I can, and I did.

All these situations have increased my confidence and courage to use my voice for others and myself. During Covid, I had a senior role as head of change management in a boutique consulting firm. We had a tremendous workload, a duplication in the workforce and turnover, and an old-school micromanaging leadership. Initially, my dream role was growing a team, defining a new solution, and offering and deciding the related business strategy. Over time, I became frustrated with the reality of being micromanaged. Taking care of client projects, coaching young consultants, particularly women, and building a network for women were very important to me. It gave me visibility not only inside of the company but also outside. During a crucial conversation with my boss, we discussed my career and work situation. He was pleased with my achievements and results, but I saw no career promotions soon. "Maybe in 5 years, I could take over his role when he retires."

Instead, I quit. I had never left without a new contract before. But I knew, by now, I could take risks with my reputation, experience, and network. The essential parts to growing a consulting business are "experience" and "network." Some clients told me that I could come back anytime. The clients who knew I dared to handle difficult situations and defend a "no." The network I had built over the last 22 years who knew me. But more importantly, I was courageous enough to reach out to them for new opportunities. And an outstanding opportunity as a member of the board of an investment fund came around the corner. Scary, exciting, and unique. Today, I am super proud to have jumped into the unknown.

I am striving to share my experiences with other women in consulting. I love this industry – the dynamic, the drive, the daringness. There are infinite opportunities to learn new things, develop inspiring solutions for your customers, and grow personally and as part of a business. Yes, there are career challenges to balancing work and life, despite the reduced levels of travel and the increased work-time flexibilities that the pandemic has initiated. Men still predominantly take on decision-making roles in consulting. However, clients increasingly demand diverse consulting teams to mimic their workforce or customer base. They know that the level of innovation is higher and the results are better with diverse groups. Consulting companies I have worked for have already lost contracts because of a lack of team diversity. Hence the number of opportunities for women to create and craft their careers and balanced working conditions in consulting is increasing.

So, what does it take?

My three key pieces of advice for women in consulting are:

✦ Be Clear: Know precisely what you stand for and what you want. Identify your core values and write down what you exactly want and how you want to feel at the end of the day/the year. (Listing everything you don't like does not mean you want the opposite. Be specific and clear).

✦ Be Confident: Know your subject (your subject matter expertise) and the value you bring to your firm, your network, and your clients. Create your own value proposition.

✦ Be Courageous: Speak up and take a leap of faith. What would you do if you were not afraid? And most of all: Have fun!

These 3Cs (Clarity, Confidence, Courage) are the cornerstones of my accelerator program "WomenLoveConsulting." It is designed to fit into a consulting life. It works for mid-sized consulting firms as their "external accelerator program" for their female talents.

This program has helped female consultants:

1. Clearly sharpened their USP (unique selling proposition)

2. Confidently build a strong network and

3. Courageously developed a profitable business case for their next promotion.

The "WomenLoveConsulting Accelerator Program" is six months of weekly:

✦ Content,

✦ Group coaching,

✦ Role plays,

✦ Networking, and

✦ Implementation to ensure sustainable results.

If you want to know more about how I can help your firm or how this program will fit into your setup, just reach out to me, and let's have a conversation.

Contact me via email: hello@ineskaps.com or https://www.linkedin.com/in/ineskaps/

www.ineskaps.com

My mission is to empower women to create their best careers and reach the top in management consulting.

Being all that is possible, – first of all, is being curious.

# Finding Your Inner Butterfly

## By Katie Jordan

K atie Jordan is a certified Life Coach based in Denver, with over 20 years of experience helping women rediscover their inner butterflies. She is the creator of The Butterfly Tribe Blueprint a unique Lifestyle Coaching Program that helps divorced or single women, create a ripple effect by helping other women. The Butterfly Tribe Blueprint helps create a roadmap toward clarity for the next steps in 30 days or less. With newfound confidence to not care too much what other people think, trusting themselves enough to make decisions, and feeling worthy of living the life they dream of.

It is time to break out of the cocoon life has put you in, spread your wings, and fly!

**Contact Katie:**

LinkedIn: www.linkedin.com/in/butterflytribeblueprint

Facebook: https://www.facebook.com/groups/butterflytribeblueprint/

Instagram: https://instagram.com/butterflytribeblueprint?igshid=ZDdkNTZiNTM=

Website: www.butterflytribeblueprint.com

# Finding Your
# Inner Butterfly
# By Katie Jordan

here is an innate need and will for us to achieve more. The desire to achieve more is not for monetary gain, self-righteousness, or ego but to make a sustainable impact that will have a lasting effect. We accomplish this through the mindset we create, the boundaries we enforce, and the self-awareness to extend ourselves grace.

Have you ever felt there is more to life? Trust me. You are not alone. There is an internal flame and drive. A drive that can push people to be successful early on or push them into what society thinks they should do, such as going to school, getting married and having a family. For some, this buries what they want, causing them to lose their identity.

I was somewhere in the middle of these two. I knew I always wanted more, but I couldn't quite figure out what that was. Little did I know this journey would take me from being a caterpillar to emerging as a beautiful, strong, and bold butterfly. I had an entrepreneurial spirit from the early stages of being a caterpillar. I started selling wrapping paper at a young age. I always had a steady job, and I held two positions while in college. I continued to feel that there was more.

I was a caterpillar watching the butterfly, knowing that one day that was where I was going to be. Unsure of how I was getting there. I tried selling supplements, kitchen gadgets, and make-up and was even known as Katie the Bling Lady, hoping this would fill that desire for a bigger purpose. Instead, I was left wondering what I was doing. None of these things fulfilled that burning desire in me for more. Through a lengthy process of learning and life lessons, I would discover my true calling. I was a caterpillar going into a cocoon through life's storms.

Becoming a butterfly did not happen overnight; it was a process. Life was good. I lived in San Diego and had a great corporate job. Riding my bike and volunteering was a big part of my life. Even though I was happy, there was still this little pull inside me, wanting more. At the age of 36, I got married. I was in a much better position and understanding of marriage than others. Little did I know I was very wrong about this. I was disadvantaged here because I didn't know my inner being. The inner person who could hold space for themselves and another person as they grow and evolve.

In 2016 we experienced a devastating miscarriage. Working through the pain and the emotion of this was not easy. A year later, I experienced one of the biggest joys in my life–the birth of my daughter. This little person has taught me so much through the journey of motherhood. I strongly desired to do better for her and give her opportunities because I better understood life.

The same year my daughter was born, in 2017, I lost my grandmother, and then in 2018, I got a phone call from my oldest sister Jovie saying our father had passed. Jovie would start having seizures the following year only to learn she had brain cancer. In April and May of 2020, I would drive 3 hours to see her every week until she lost her battle. She passed very early in the morning, and I remember being with her children, hearing a bird sing, and knowing she was no longer in pain. I was devastated to lose my sister at such a young age. She was one of my biggest cheerleaders.

One of the ways I was able to honor her was by giving her Eulogy. Stepping out of the van, I remember like it was yesterday, thinking I was not the 15-year-old girl most people remember. I have evolved into this amazing butterfly who has experienced life and the many things it offers. I want them to see me for who I have become, not who I was as a young woman. I vividly remember one night lying in bed, my heart feeling like it was breaking into a million pieces wondering how people survive through this amount of grief.

At that point, I knew I had two choices. I could stay in the cocoon of grief and isolate myself from those around me, or I could find a way to evolve with that grief and not allow it to be all-consuming. As I started breaking out of the cocoon, the right opportunities emerged. One of my leaders at work shared with me the life transformation she was going through. Her story piqued my interest, and I started looking into different opportunities for personal growth. For my birthday, I gifted myself a ticket to the World Summitt. I had no idea what I was getting myself into. I just trusted that it was going to be amazing. One of the main things I learned was the importance of mindset.

I viewed myself as a positive person, which was true. Mindset is not just about being positive or negative but about how you view the world. Do you take the negative things and look for the positives, or do you allow them to harden you?

I started with the transformation by creating a morning routine of gratitude journaling and working out. I would get up earlier than anyone else in the house. At first, this was challenging, and I had to experiment with doing things in different ways. When you start to put together your routine, be flexible and realize that if something is not bringing you happiness, you can always change how you do things. I went from morning gratitude journaling and working out to meditation, gratitude journaling, and "I am" statements. As I continue to grow, my morning routine evolves as well. How you complete your routine may differ, but the important part is that you are taking steps to make the changes.

Starting my day with gratitude gives me a different perspective on the day. Creating this shift allows me to be a better Mom, family member, friend, and leader. I now approach situations with the mindset that everyone has a story. Some are painful, and others are joyful. Viewing conditions this way allows me to show empathy and compassion.

Meditation also became something I started doing as well. For me, it was not about emptying my mind. It was about bringing it back to self. Currently, I start my days with at least 10 minutes of meditation. You don't have to be in meditation for long periods for it to be impactful. Sometimes we allow ourselves to stay in a co-coon because we let fear take over, not doing something because it is different. What will others think? I can't clear my mind. I can't even remember what I am supposed to be doing. Meditation is not about doing it perfectly. It is about showing up and trying. Just like muscles, the more you exercise them, the more defined they get. The continuous steps allow the butterfly to escape the cocoon, and we must continue forward momentum.

As I continued to shift my mindset, I realized I had been giving my power away. I relinquished my control by failing to set boundar-ies, which made me feel trapped in my cocoon. As I started to under-stand the importance of having boundaries with myself and others, I started enforcing them. I started practicing this by saying no to the things I didn't want to do. Was that hard in the beginning? Yes, I was a people pleaser by nature. I believed I would be satisfied if I were making others happy. That was the furthest thing from the truth. I did not know where that line was, so I said yes to everything, even if it was something I didn't want to do. I thought the expectations were not because I wanted to. Part of not knowing who I was came from catering to others, losing, and not paying attention to myself. I did not realize that self-care was not selfish. It was the opposite. Part of self-care is setting boundaries with myself and taking back the power I so freely gave way. Setting a boundary that works for yourself also requires knowing yourself. For me, that is a continuous journey and does not stop.

Part of knowing myself was recognizing different patterns in my life and doing the inner work to change them. One of those patterns was my self-doubt, not thinking I was good enough or worthy of living the life of my dreams. Part of that was recognizing where those thoughts stemmed from, acknowledging that, and letting it go. Journaling was a great place for this because I could ask myself why. I was always taking care of what I thought was taking care of others and not doing the same for myself. Changing this didn't come over-night; it took therapy and work. Through this, I have learned what it means to love myself and how to love others.

The awareness I learned was an essential step in becoming a butterfly. Knowing things are always working out for me, even when they don't feel like it. Once I was conscious of the changes I needed to make in my life, my self-awareness journey started. I began to see many different things in my life that needed to change for myself and those around me. I recognized patterns and old behaviors and made conscious decisions to react differently. Previously Katie would have shut down in difficult conversations. Today's Katie listens for understanding, responding from a place of kindness and compassion.

I started joining women in business groups virtually. In one of these groups, I met a woman named Danielle Gray. She was working a full-time job and launching a business at the time. I was drawn to her work because I wanted to do that. I started following her journey, joining her amazing group of women. As I watched her journey, I thought I could do this too. I was becoming increasingly aware of the different things that had to change for me to spread my wings and fly.

During the spring of the following year, one of my dear friends, Lina, was doing an online challenge called Reawaken the Champion Within with Dave Scatchard, an ex-NHL player. His program was where I learned a lot about the reprogramming of old thoughts and patterns. The online challenge was super powerful because I was starting to see how things in my past affected the present and where I was going.

Being aware can change the way you look at things and move forward. Even after this change, there are still days when the cocoon tries to creep in. Is it rainbows and sunshine everyday? No, but when you have the awareness and mental space coupled with firm boundaries, you can recognize, acknowledge, and be better prepared to release them and move forward with much more ease and grace.

I had to go through all these things to be in the right place to realize my purpose. Life lessons are complicated, and sometimes we don't see why when we are in them. It is about taking those lessons, helping others spread their wings, and becoming the butterfly you are.

Through a lengthy process of cocoon building, I discovered my true calling, emerging through life's storms as a beautiful butterfly. I had to spend time in the cocoon life put me in to grow and discover the wings I have to fly. My purpose is to help others find their wings and fly.

Join me, and together, let's create a kaleidoscope of women who support each other, spread our wings and fly!

www.butterflytribeblueprint.com

Butterfly Tribe Blueprint Facebook Group

LinkedIn: www.linkedin.com/in/butterflytribeblueprint

Insta: @ButterflyTribeBlueprint

# Turn Your Pain into Power

## By Summer Montabone

Summer Montabone is the CEO & Founder of Summer's Fitness Inc. and Summer Montabone Coaching & Consulting.

As a multi-passionate entrepreneur with over 29 years' experience, she has worn many titles, including: personal trainer, health educator, leader, mom, retired pro athlete, elite coach, trauma survivor, and CEO. Summer has leveraged her expertise in the world of health & fitness and business ownership to create a step-by-step formula that helps women feel, do, and achieve their personal best.

Summer has been invited as a contributing expert to speak and write for organizations such as the Functional Aging Summit, International Society of Sports Nutrition, and Oxygen magazine. Summer is a highly awarded professional, having earned the Women's

Impact Award, Circle of Excellence, Presidents Circle, and Best of Canton Business awards.

After hitting rock bottom with postpartum depression, Summer regained control of her life and set out on a mission to empower women to become fearless decision makers and CEOs of their own lives! Summer lives in Ohio with her husband, two school age daughters, and their cat and cavapoo.

**Contact Summer:**

LinkedIn: https://www.linkedin.com/in/summermontabone/

Facebook: https://www.facebook.com/summer.stevenhagenmontabone/

Facebook: https://www.facebook.com/SummerMontabone1

Instagram: @summermontabone

Website: www.summermontabone.com

# Turn Your Pain
# into Power
# By Summer Montabone

*"I believe women have been conditioned to be sick, stuck, and hurt. I also believe, no matter what hardships you have faced or are facing now; you have the power to become a fearless decision-maker and the CEO of your life. As the CEO of your own life, you can create harmony with your family, health, and career or business, in any season of life."*
~ Summer Montabone

I've always been an entrepreneur and a high achiever. In 5th grade, because my parents would not let us get a pet, I started a dog-walking business: *"Seasons Pet Care - Summer, Winter, Spring or Fall: All You Have To Do Is Call!"* In 7th grade, I volunteered to shovel horse stalls, and eventually rode and showed horses. After high school, I went on to earn my Bachelor's in Education. Once I completed college, my husband and I married and decided to move back to our hometown. After dealing with what I thought were "sleep issues", I decided not to look for a teaching job. Instead, I took a part-time job as a fitness attendant at a local YMCA making $8 per hour.

Within two months of giving free fitness orientations at the YMCA, I had built up a clientele of personal training clients and was "limited" to recording 29 hours a week on my time card; despite putting in 50+ hours a week as an employee. The YMCA literally did not know what to do with me ;) Back in 2003 personal trainers weren't doing small group personal training and teaching "bootcamp classes". This was natural to me due to my teaching background.

Small group training was also a more affordable "solution" for people to invest in personal training to reach their goals.

After 2 years of trying to get the YMCA on board with my ideas for growing personal training, all I kept hearing was "no you can't do that". With encouragement from a client, I DECIDED to go out on my own. I worked out an arrangement to start a personal training business at a local gym.

**I was told, by many, I would "never make a living as a personal trainer".**

It was natural to me during my time at the YMCA to collect email addresses and send a weekly email newsletter with updates and education to the clients. *I love to teach, empower, & educate!* Little did I know I was "email marketing".

I had built a list of 1500 names on my email list, wrote articles and submitted my own press releases to the local newspapers, and was able to grow a personal training business; *even with no degree or formal education in marketing or business.*

In the fall of 2004, I went out on my own as a personal trainer. It was the perfect timing as I made the DECISION *before* I took 1st place at the 2004 NPC Fitness Nationals earning IFBB Professional Athlete status. This "girl" from a small town in Ohio was even flown to LA to be featured in a national fitness magazine. These were two more things I was told "you'll never be able to do that".

I spent two years at that local gym and was quickly outgrowing the space for my vision of personal training. I brought on two part-time personal trainers; coaching, mentoring and employing (paying & investing in) them. I was a business owner and "thought" I was ready for my own physical or brick & mortar location.

## THE DAY I HAD A HEART ATTACK

I was so scared to go out on my own! The financial risk was HUGE! I literally thought I was having a heart attack, on September 27, 2007, when I signed my life away to rent the 6,000-square-foot space. *I had to sign personally.* It was ALL my responsibility and it was my reputation to succeed and make it work. My husband supported me, but at the end of the day, it was all me. Many would make comments and assumptions that as a female I had help from my parents, my spouse, or even the bank.

I have always considered myself proactive. I had saved up enough money that I only needed a loan for the $100,000+ in equipment to outfit the space. I also didn't pay myself for a couple of years before opening what is known today as the Summer's Fitness Inc. location.

**I made sacrifices for a bigger vision.**

Before signing the lease to open the space, I invested in a local Women's Business Coach who came highly recommended. I continued working with her, in a group, for 9 years. I eventually overlapped with a Fitness Business Coach I invested in, too.

For the first 3 years I brought home $15,000 a year, even though I was working 60+ hours a week building every aspect of the business; and still getting my own fitness workouts in. That breaks down to about $5 an hour to pour your heart and soul into building something to make a bigger impact on others.

**Surround yourself with like-minded people and invest in coaching and mentorship.**

According to the IHRSA, **81 percent** of health and fitness studios fail within their first year. The fact I was bringing home any money was a win.

I had the vision to create a space for people to get an education and be a part of a community. "Achieve Your Personal Best!" ® is the tagline we have had since 2007 and is still on the walls of the studio today. It was something I BELIEVED in and had a VISION for. I was willing to dedicate my life and resources to helping people improve their lives for the better.

*Achieve Your Personal Best!* ® For me it was and has been, bigger than just a gym.

## MOTHERHOOD

Three years after opening my fitness studio, one of the athletes I coached WON a TOP International competition and my business continued to grow locally and internationally. I had the opportunity to coach women, online, all around the country and the world. I was coaching online even before it was a thing. I like to say that in some ways I've always been ahead of the curve - which the curve later presented in 2020, as you know.

In 2011, after 12 years of marriage, I had my first child and embarked on motherhood as a mom, without a mom. I was in a new season of life as a "CEO Mom" and my life was turned upside down. When my daughter was 5 weeks old, I was admitted to the hospital.

*How could someone so strong and "accomplished" find themselves in a physiatric unit for a week?*

*Can anyone ever amount to anything after a mental health crisis?*

I am the oldest of 6 children and was always the "rock" of the family. At this time; I had hit rock bottom.

I knew I was going to have to dig deep and use the same strong belief and mindset skills I had learned as a pro athlete and successful business owner, to embark on this new journey of self-care to regain control of my health & happiness. I became a fanatical study in self-development working with doctors, counselors, mentors, and coaches.

## DECIDE, CREATE, and EVOLVE AGAIN

In 2014, we welcomed our 2nd daughter. I did things A LOT differently and invested in support as a CEO Mom, at home, and in my business.

I started having mixed feelings about the physique competitor/athlete aspect of the business. It just wasn't in my heart or what I was passionate about anymore. It had become a 6-figure online business in 12 months, with women flying in from all over the world to train with me. I was referred to as the "iconic" coach, and I had coached the one and only 3x World Champion– but it still didn't feel right.

**Business opportunities will present, but personal alignment is more important.**

One day, a woman was in my office crying because she hadn't yet won a "sword" (a type of trophy) at a contest. I thought to myself, "this isn't a real problem". I decided that day, I no longer wanted to use my gifts to help women win trophies, but to **empower women, especially moms, to become their own personal champions and CEO of their own Life!**

So, I closed down a 6 figure online business and stopped training competitors. My mission and vision for health and fitness looked different. Of course, a lot of people did not like MY DECISION. It temporarily impacted my business, negatively, as I set out to evolve into our next season of business and life.

My renewed vision was to empower women to stop pretending they are happy and going through the motions of life. I recognized that many women are carrying the weight of the world on their shoulders and it is showing up on their waists. I knew striving for "weight loss" was a symptom of something deeper. I was on a mission to create a safe space and a realistic solution to this problem.

**I believed in myself, did the personal development work, and invested in trusted coaches and mentors.**

Move on and upward. It doesn't matter what anyone thinks. No business owner wants to lose money, but if you are confident in your leadership you can build and grow again. I survive and thrive, I always do. I am a warrior mom and that life experience coupled with a growth mindset takes me far, *and it will you, too.* When you have clarity, confidence, and purpose you become a fearless decision-maker and the CEO of your life and business.

You are going to be faced with an entrepreneurial roller coaster. *Enjoy the ride!*

I now look at challenges as opportunities for better solutions and more growth. I welcome them and prepare for them.

## THE NEXT SEASON TO EVOLVE - CLOSE THE GAP

Reading books, and working with coaches, counselors, and mentors to overcome personal and professional pains; I recognized there was a *gap for women*, especially moms, who have a career or business. Based on the obstacles faced and goals crushed; I created a framework and course and launched the CEO Moms Mentorship which I now call

*Fearless Academy for Women.* I combined an education platform: video lessons, easy-to-follow worksheets, and a Call to Action assignment, with group coaching & accountability and 1 on 1 coaching.

The success stories from the women, who have driven women with demanding careers or businesses, typically moms whether school-age kids or empty nesters, *were amazing!*

Women who started their own businesses, women executives receiving **25% salary increases** and more time off, women losing as much as 68 pounds, but the theme was consistent - women who now felt CONFIDENT in the way they feel, look, and use their voice.

The magic happens on our 1 on 1 coaching calls, but women no longer feel alone supported by a community of other now Fearless Women!

Ultimately, I recognized you need to become a fearless decision-maker and CEO of your own life before you can truly be an effective "CEO" or leader in your career or business. You can find harmony with your family, health, and career or business to unleash your full potential and achieve your personal best! ®

**This is my purpose. When you live and work in your zone of genius; you are fulfilled. You can make an impact and an income.**

Leveraging over 25+ years as a coach, teacher, and successful business owner and experiencing pain to overcome obstacles; I recognized my personal and professional power and I want to help other women do the same.

*"Summer sees potential in people."*

*"Summer has a gift as a life coach and professional coach. I thought this would be the same as anything else I've tried, but Summer proved me wrong. I have come out of this with a totally different mindset - in my personal life and in my career."*

Just because someone has an MBA doesn't mean they know how to run a business. Just because someone has the title "Coach" doesn't mean they are effective.

## FACED WITH THE CURVE = PAUSE

Running a business is hard. Overseeing a team of employees is hard. Being a parent is hard.

Those are challenging enough on their own, and now I was adding a new "online" business! I was excited, *but then 2020 hit!*

I had to jump back into the fitness studio and have a more hands-on role as CEO, as this was uncharted territory for everyone. We didn't skip a beat and we evolved in delivering fitness coaching virtually, but we also lost over 25% of our revenue overnight. All this tested my leadership and meant I had to pause my efforts for Fearless Academy for Women.

**You will be faced with a start, stop, start, pause, and start again.**

Women are superheroes and supermoms, but we only have so much energy to give. We have to know when it's time to take a pause in both our personal and professional life. We have to know how to prioritize and delegate. This is exactly what I teach at Fearless Academy.

## WE MADE IT! OR DID WE?

During 2020 and 2021 I watched many of my rockstar peers from fitness masterminds close their physical fitness locations, *permanently*.

Celebrating 15 years of Summer's Fitness Inc. was a huge milestone, especially with the impact of COVID on the fitness industry, with many gyms shutting down.

As a fitness studio owner, despite losing over 25% of our revenue immediately, I was able to retain ALL of my staff during 2020 and beyond. We are stable, but it CONTINUES to be challenging. Behind-the-scenes challenges that ONLY business owners can fully understand.

I wasn't the only one facing hardships. My husband's hospital closed in 2018 and he lost his job.

By 2020 I had a medication-induced 40-pound weight gain. I did a deep dive and lost 35 pounds by 2022 and then faced another personal challenge; a cancer scare and a complete hysterectomy including my ovaries. In 2023 my fitness studio general manager resigned.

**You will be tested. You will feel alone. You have to become a fearless decision-maker and the CEO of your life and business; whether that means stepping up or walking away.**

Evolve and evolve again.

## CONNECTION and SUPPORT

Throughout my journey as a multifaceted woman, mom, trauma survivor, pro-athlete, entrepreneur, and business owner, I have embraced every painful moment as a lesson learned. It wasn't always that way early on.

The biggest thing I recognized is you need the RIGHT SUPPORT who can relate to both your personal challenges and professional challenges. That doesn't mean excuses; as *personal responsibility is key*.

**I would LOVE to connect with you and offer you support on your journey to:**

GAIN CLARITY

STRENGTHEN CONFIDENCE

DISCOVER PURPOSE

UNLOCK PERSONAL POWER

LIVE FEARLESSLY

Become a fearless decision-maker and CEO of your life!

Please visit my website https://summermontabone.com/suso-bookfreegift and download my *11 Steps for Becoming a Fearless Decision Maker and CEO of your life!*

Please connect with me on social media: @summermontabone

Facebook, Instagram, Linked In

I look forward to learning more about you and your goals, too!

# The Power of Persistence: Overcoming the Hurdles of Entrepreneurship

*By Jocelyn Galicia Powell*

ocelyn Galicia Powell is a 26 year old American business woman. She started her first business as a Freshman at Wichita State University at the age of 19. She now owns 6 different businesses along with her husband, Connor. These include an auto detailing shop, restaurant, convenience store, school, marketing service, and real estate holding company. She was a contestant on season 2 and 6 of The Blox, the world's largest live in entrepreneurship competition. Her accolades include being finalist for Midwest Student Entrepreneur of the Year and being chosen as Wichita's 5 under 25. In her spare time, Jocelyn speaks at business conferences and events. She also loves to coach other entrepreneurs. Jocelyn is due with her first child in 2023 and is very excited to become a mom. She is also an animal lover and fosters kittens for an animal rescue organization.

**Contact Jocelyn:**

LinkedIn: www.linkedin.com/in/jocelyngaliciapowell

Facebook: https://www.facebook.com/JocelynGaliciaPowell/

Instagram: https://www.instagram.com/joyfuljocy/

Website: https://jocelynpowell.com/

# The Power of Persistence: Overcoming the Hurdles of Entrepreneurship
## By Jocelyn Galicia Powell

"Should I just give up? This business will never work if I'm doing it alone," I thought to myself as I tried for hours to fall asleep on a school night. These thoughts of self-doubt would dance in my brain until I finally fell asleep.

I was 20 and I had just started my first business along with two of my cousins. They wanted to close the business. It was interfering with their classwork and their goals of becoming engineers. The business was growing quickly and we were new to the business world. Our new mobile mechanic business was called Mobile Car Tune. We had serviced our 100th customer in less than 3 months. For three young college students, that was incredible.

I knew that I wanted to become a serial entrepreneur since I was 12 years old, but I never thought my first business would be a mobile mechanic business. I always thought I would choose something girly. I knew nothing about cars. Zilch. How could I possibly run this business without my cousins and their abundant mechanical knowledge?

So much self-doubt filled my mind. A woman is supposed to take care of the household and cook, not run a car business. That was what my Mexican culture taught me. My parents immigrated to the U.S. from Mexico with nothing but clothes on their backs. They made sacrifices for their family and I am grateful to them for doing the best they could to raise me. However, the difference between American culture and Mexican culture was an obstacle I had to emotionally endure. My lust for independence caused a lot of tension between my parents and me growing up. Although difficult, this caused me to develop a hunger to prove that I could become something in life. A little voice that loves to do the risky thing even when my inner self-doubt voice gets loud. I owe my success to her. That little quiet voice believes that I am capable of anything. Although she scares me, I listen to her. I continued with the business alone.

The first few months of being on my own were defeating. I was studying Entrepreneurship at the time so I had an understanding of business concepts and I had customers, but I needed quality mechanics to perform the services. I had to hire a team. The difficulty in hiring a team presented itself very quickly. As someone who did not understand how a car worked, I couldn't vet the service providers correctly. I was also the person answering phone calls which I quickly realized I was unqualified for. I had so many questions and unknowns that I felt like quitting and starting over would be easier. That doubt was creeping in again.

## Lesson #1

*Through these mental challenges, I extracted my first big lesson in entrepreneurship. You are constantly encountering problems and challenges. They come in all different forms, whether they are growing pains, lack of labor, low sales, personal hurdles, etc. Every single day proves to be different and full of highs and lows. I needed to learn to regulate my emotions as I navigated the day-to-day tasks of running my business. Over time, I worked to not get worked up. Now, I can tackle day-to-day problems with solutions and not let it affect my overall mental health. It took time to get there but this has helped me now run 6 different businesses and be happier than ever.*

I started immediately hiring and building a network of professionals that I could ask questions. I didn't have all the answers but I was determined to find them. I finally had a functioning business and I was a full-time university student.

## Lesson #2

*Around this time I realized that it is so important to have the right people in the right roles. Myself, the business owner, included. Some business owners thrive on providing the services and outsourcing marketing, accounting, etc. to someone else. For me, I love working ON the business and not IN the business. I see myself as someone who is putting puzzle pieces together. Each piece represents one moving part (social media, customer service, bookkeeping, etc.). I put the right people doing the right roles together and oversee that the pieces stay in place. I have found that this allows me to focus more on improvements, growth, and building a portfolio of diverse businesses.*

I worked hard to keep the business running until I graduated with an Entrepreneurship and Real Estate degree in 2018. I was part of the first generation in my family to attain a college degree and the first woman. It was a great feeling. Plus, now I could dedicate myself to building my business full-time. The pieces felt like they were falling into place.

I finally had time on my hands but I needed to figure out how to grow the business. I joined a business accelerator program and a mentorship program. I did as much networking as I could find to meet others in the business community. This opened so many doors for me. I found an investor, mentors, clients, and a support network.

## Lesson #3

*It is important to surround yourself with people who want to see you succeed. Meet as many people as possible. Offer them support and value and you will get that in return.*

My little business was growing and now had the right resources surrounding it. We still had a lot to figure out though. The ultimate goal was to build Uber for car maintenance. At this point, we had serviced a large variety of vehicles and determined that long-term and at scale, there are too many variables that could go wrong. The mobile mechanic service business was not viable in the way we were doing it. I added mobile detailing as a service in order to test whether that service might work better.

It felt like every time I solved a problem another one was created.

## Lesson #4

*What helped get me through these moments was learning from other business owners and realizing that no one has all the answers. Especially when you are building a new concept and innovating within an industry. We are all doing the best we can and learning as we go. We are more like scientists doing experiments until we find the right solution. It is the Build, Measure, Learn framework.*

In retrospect, the most challenging times of my life have been the ones where I have grown the most. The challenging times in business have felt low at the moment, but they have led to pivots that changed the trajectory of my business for the better. They have made me think outside the box.

This is what happened in 2018 when we added mobile detailing as a service. It quickly became 70% of our sales and 5% of our headaches. The numbers were telling me that it was time to pivot. It was a big decision to cut out the mechanic services which we had started with. It was scary but at the end of the day, I made a data-driven decision, not an emotionally driven decision. The numbers didn't lie. We cut out mechanic services and started to fully focus on detailing.

After pivoting to mobile auto detailing and finding an investor in 2019, we started growing significantly. We started working with large companies to clean their fleets and added auto-cleaning subscriptions. The subscriptions are like a regular housekeeper but for your car. We help busy people stay proud of the car they drive. By performing our service in the car owner's driveway, we save car owners from lines, waiting rooms, and inconvenient trips to drop off their car at a shop. Cars are parked 95% of the time. It just makes more sense for service providers to come to the car.

I had great plans for 2020 and then the COVID pandemic hit. During the first few weeks of the pandemic, our sales dwindled to just a few hundred dollars per week. It was very painful to feel like something I worked so hard to build was coming undone and I had no control over it. I took time to process what was happening and created a cash preservation plan. Thankfully I had just spent the last year finding the most cost-effective way to detail a car without compromising the quality. I had positioned the business to have very low fixed costs and high variable costs that fluctuate depending on the amount of business we have. Over time I extracted lessons to improve our service and processes. Our fixed expenses were as low as they could get. I had to go many months without pay but the business stayed alive.

## Lesson #5

*Business can be unpredictable. Even when things are out of your control you still have control over some variables. Work on those to mitigate your losses. In the wise words of my investor "sometimes the only decision we can make is the least bad decision."*

I spent 2020 - 2021 adjusting to the new norm like everyone else. Business slowly started coming back. We gained all the customers we had lost at the beginning of the pandemic and added even more.

I made sure to build the business in a way that didn't involve me in the day-to-day operations. My goal with any business I own is to build it to work without me as much as possible. That allowed me the freedom to seek out other business opportunities.

In 2021, I married another serial entrepreneur. He and I operated different businesses so we both came in with different experiences and knowledge. That really helps us work together as a team. We are serial entrepreneurs at heart and we love to evaluate new business opportunities. Together, we have started or purchased 6 different businesses and look forward to growing our portfolio over our lifetime.

## Lesson #6

*Don't let ideas and opportunities that are not worth it distract you from your primary revenue stream/business. When an opportunity presents itself, evaluate it using data and be real with yourself. How much time is this going to take? Is it realistic? Is it financially worth it? Would your time be more valuable being spent on your primary revenue stream/business instead of the new opportunity?*

Some opportunities that have come across our desk have not been worth pursuing long-term. We learned that the hard way. Over time, we have learned to ask ourselves better questions and evaluate business opportunities more efficiently.

Now, we own a detailing business (2U AUTO), a restaurant, a convenience store, an affiliate marketing company, a commercial real estate investment portfolio, and a school.

I love the day-to-day of checking in on our businesses. Every single day is different. It presents new challenges and new wins. We get to work with our amazing teams and watch them thrive in their roles. We have the most amazing business partners that enable us to use our strengths and fill in where we have weaknesses. We are serial entrepreneurs at heart and we don't plan on slowing down.

## Lesson #7

*If you're thinking about starting a business, do it! The quicker you start, the quicker you'll get to where you want to be! You've got this!*

There are so many other lessons to learn. I hope that you found some value in my story and that you never stop learning.

I have also found a passion for helping other business owners grow personally and professionally. You can reach me through my website www.jocelynpowell.com and follow me on Instagram @joyfuljocy. Thank you for reading. Best wishes!

# Breaking Free and Starting Over: A Journey to Emotional Mastery

## By Rashda Shanaz

ashda Shanaz is a successful entrepreneur, author, and coach specializing in helping ambitious women achieve their goals. With a background in healthcare and people management, plus a passion for personal development, she has built a reputation for delivering practical and effective strategies that empower women to take control of their careers and lives.

Through her coaching programs, books, and speaking engagements, Rashda has helped countless women overcome their fears, break through barriers, and succeed on their terms. Her unique approach combines the latest NLP and timeline therapy techniques with real-world experience and a healthy dose of humor.

Whether you're looking to launch your business, climb the corporate ladder, or simply take your life to the next level, Rashda has the tools and expertise to help you. With her guidance, you can unleash your full potential and create the life you've always dreamed of.

**Contact Rashda:**

LinkedIn: https://www.linkedin.com/in/rashda-shanaz-656ab220/

Facebook: https://www.facebook.com/rashda.shanaz

Instagram: @rashda_coach_transform_travel

Website: https://rashdashanaz.wixsite.com/rashdashanaz

# Breaking Free and Starting Over: A Journey to Emotional Mastery
## By Rashda Shanaz

I was born into a typical British Pakistani household in the '80s in inner-city Birmingham. Being the 6th daughter and 7th child overall out of 8 children, you can imagine that by the time I came around, my parents were just like, "Oh, another one? Let's just stick her in the assembly line with the others." But little do they know, I'm made for more than just being a clone of my older sisters.

Growing up in a typical British Pakistani household, I am supposed to conform to the roles assigned to me by my family's expectations and our society. However, I felt unfulfilled and unhappy in this role. To make matters worse, my mother constantly pitted her daughters against each other and was the primary source of the narcissistic abuse that existed within our family. Even though this abuse also spread to other extended family members, no one seemed willing to step in and help. As a result, I felt trapped and unsure of how to break free from the constraints holding me back.

As I pursued my dreams, I lacked the support of my family. Despite the toxic environment at home, I always hoped my sisters would support me. After all, they had both managed to escape the confines of our family's expectations and establish their paths. They were against whatever success I was trying to achieve. I couldn't understand why they wouldn't have my back, especially after everything we had been through together. It wasn't until much later that I realized they had left home precisely to escape the type of scrutiny and pressure that I was still struggling to navigate. They didn't want to be pulled back into that world, and in many ways, I couldn't blame them.

Seeking support outside of the household was crucial in breaking free from the toxic dynamics within my family. However, I fell into a pattern of seeking out friends with similar traits and behaviors as my mother and sisters, ultimately impacting my emotional resilience.

For years, I continued to surround myself with people who were judgmental, critical, and quick to tear down others. I would seek their validation and approval even if it came at the cost of my emotional well-being. I was constantly on edge, wondering if I was doing enough to please them and gain acceptance. This pattern of behavior was damaging to my mental health.

Despite my efforts to seek support outside of the household, the toxicity of my family dynamics still seeps into my professional life. I landed a management position in healthcare at a remarkably young age, which should have been a source of pride and validation for my hard work and determination. Instead, one of my sisters tried to sabotage my position at work and in our family. She would make snide remarks about how I was "just a manager" and belittle my accomplishments. She seemed threatened by my success and didn't want me to thrive outside the family's control. It was a painful reminder that the emotional abuse I had experienced at home still had a hold on me, even when we were no longer living under the same roof.

It wasn't until I sought therapy and began to work on myself that I realized the importance of setting healthy boundaries and seeking out positive, supportive relationships. I learned that I could be myself and still be accepted and loved by others. It took time and effort, but I could break free from the cycle of seeking validation from toxic individuals and establish healthy relationships that lifted me and allowed me to thrive.

Despite the emotional turmoil I experienced at home, I was determined to help other women succeed. As a manager, friend, and surrogate sister, I supported those around me to the best of my ability. However, the impact of my home life on my emotional well-being was undeniable. At times, I found it challenging to focus on my work and relationships because of the constant emotional upheaval caused by my family dynamic. It was a continuous battle to maintain my professionalism and composure, even as I struggled to navigate the toxicity of my home life. Unfortunately, the dynamics of my home life did impact other areas.

As I continued to navigate the challenges of my personal and professional life, I realized that I needed fulfillment in both areas. I wanted to make a more significant impact in my community and find a career that offered me more flexibility in terms of time and location. However, as an Asian woman, my traditional path was limited to being a machinist or running a shop or takeaway. I refused to conform to these expectations and tried various other careers, including web design, training as a driving instructor, drop shipping, and counseling. However, despite my best efforts, I struggled to establish a role that would allow me to achieve my goals.

Throughout this journey, I realized I needed to work on my emotional resilience, which my upbringing and my experiences had impacted. I didn't have a coach or mentor, and this lack of support made navigating these challenges difficult. Nonetheless, I remained determined to find a path that would allow me to make a difference in the world and achieve the time and location freedom that I desired. The desire to make a difference led me down a spiritual path, allowing me to give back to my community and find fulfillment outside my work.

Although I longed to break free from the emotional turmoil at home and find a more fulfilling career, taking risks and trying new things was difficult. My working role provided a sense of stability and security that I craved in my personal life. However, even though I was successful as a healthcare manager, I still felt unfulfilled and yearned for more. I wanted to find a career that allowed me the freedom to be creative, positively impact others, and control my time and location.

However, my lack of emotional resilience and the ongoing emotional struggles in my personal life impacted each of these ventures. Without the support and guidance of a coach, it was challenging to find the motivation and confidence to pursue these opportunities with conviction. As a result, it was easy for me to remain safe in my job, even though it did not provide the sense of fulfillment I craved.

Despite my best efforts, I struggled to make ends meet and sank deeper into debt. I had exhausted all the options for making a career change without completely giving up my current profession, but nothing seemed to work out. And to make matters worse, I had no support from my friends or family. My sisters had left home to pursue their paths, leaving me feeling alone and unsupported. Though I believed I understood why they left, I couldn't help but feel a sense of resentment and isolation from them. There seemed to be no escape from the relentless loop I was in.

Despite the challenges and setbacks, I refused to give up my dream of finding fulfillment and success. I started exploring entrepreneurship, trying different ventures, and investing my time and resources. I also sought new friendships and relationships, hoping to find the support and encouragement to keep going.

At work, I continued to push myself to excel, despite the lack of support and recognition I received from my colleagues and superiors. I knew I was capable of more, and I refused to let their lack of belief in me hold me back.

Through this, I realized the key to success and fulfillment lies within me. I needed to become self-aware, emotionally resilient, and confident in myself and my abilities. I started seeking resources and mentors to help me on this journey. Slowly but surely, I started progressing, overcoming my setbacks, and building a more fulfilling life.

Despite my struggles to find my path and the lack of support from my family and friends, I refused to give up. I tried various entrepreneurial endeavors and sought fulfillment in friendships and relationships. However, I still had to juggle being an income earner and caregiver, and trying to find my way.

Despite the abuse I had suffered at the hands of my parents, I assumed the role of their primary caregiver. It was a difficult position, but I did what I could to support them while also striving to create my own fulfilling life. It wasn't easy, but I knew I wanted more and was determined to keep pushing forward.

Despite my best efforts to break free from the limitations my culture and family placed upon me, I found myself constantly comparing myself to others and their successes. My sisters, friends, and extended family thrived while I struggled to find my place. Even as I grew emotionally and spiritually, I still allowed their judgments and expectations to affect me, causing me to doubt myself and my path. It was a constant battle to stay true to myself and my dreams rather than succumbing to the pressures of conformity.

As I tried to break free from the expectations imposed on me, I was in a familiar cycle of emotional turmoil. No matter how hard I worked, I faced the same old judgments and abuse. Despite my successes as a manager and a community volunteer, I still felt unfulfilled and trapped.

The passing of my sister was a turning point for me. It was a tragedy that shook our family to the core. My father, who had always been a strong pillar in our family, struggled to continue with life. I was left to pick up the pieces. It was a time of great emotional upheaval, and my mother's narcissism was now out in full force, which had always been there simmering beneath the surface. But amid all this, I had a realization: no matter how much success you have, no matter how much you achieve, when the chips are down, nobody wants to know you. It was a sobering thought, but it was also a catalyst for change. I knew I needed to break free from the emotional chains that had been holding me back and find a way to create a truly fulfilling life.

Despite facing setbacks and challenges in my personal and professional life, I never lost sight of my desire to break free from the mold others had placed me in and achieve my full potential. I was determined to find another way, and that's when I decided to explore the world of personal development and emotional coaching.

I sometimes wondered if I was like Sisyphus, the Greek mythological figure doomed to push a boulder up a hill only to have it roll back down again. But then I remembered that Sisyphus had a trick up his sleeve. He had the power to choose how he reacted to his situation.

So I took a page from Sisyphus's book and changed my reaction. I stopped trying to fit into the mold created for me and started living life on my terms. I embraced my passion for entrepreneurship and took steps to establish my own business. I sought out new friendships and relationships that were supportive and empowering. And I consciously tried to distance myself from the toxic people in my life, even if they were family.

It wasn't an easy road, but it was worth it. Breaking free from the expectations of others allowed me to find my path and live a truly fulfilling life.

I realized that the key to unlocking my potential was to master my emotions and achieve emotional resilience. Through my journey of personal development and working with a life coach and transformational coach, I learned the importance of emotional mastery and strength and how to apply these skills to my own life and help others.

As I continued my journey of self-discovery and personal growth, I realized that helping others break free from the limiting beliefs and cultural expectations that held them back was my true calling. I started my own coaching business, focusing on emotional mastery, and saw incredible transformations in the women I coached. Many of them are held back by the same societal and cultural pressures that I had faced, and I was able to guide them toward a new level of understanding and self-awareness. With these newfound skills, I was able to help my friends and family members achieve emotional mastery and establish appropriate boundaries with those who did not want to accept me for who I was.

As I helped these women break free from their old patterns and beliefs, I also continued to build my own life of freedom. I started a travel business that allowed me to work from anywhere, and I was finally able to become debt-free. It was a long and challenging road, but I was able to create a life of my design, free from the constraints of cultural expectations and other people's judgments.

Becoming an emotional mastery coach was the natural progression for me, as I had experienced first-hand the power of emotional resilience and self-awareness in breaking free from the limiting beliefs that had held me back for so long. Now, I could share my knowledge and experience with others, empowering them to create the lives they truly wanted.

Becoming a coach and mastering emotional intelligence allowed me to transform my life, help other women break free from cultural limitations, and build a life of freedom. I aim to use Neuro Linguistic Programming and timeline therapy to help others live, travel, and pray wherever they want, without limitations.

I hope you have connected with my story and will continue to do so via the services I offer at https://rashdashanaz.wixsite.com/rashdashanaz and follow me on Facebook: https://www.facebook.com/rashda.shanaz, Instagram: https://www.instagram.com/rashda_coach_transform_travel/, LinkedIn: https://www.linkedin.com/in/rashda-shanaz-656ab220/ and Twitter: https://twitter.com/Rshanaz1980

# Arriving Right on Time

## By LeAnn Lazar

eAnn Lazar is an LA-based Divorce, Dating and Co-Parenting expert and a certified NLP practitioner. Eloquently coined the "life sorter" by friends and colleagues she knew her path was to help others create their best life. LeAnn is passionate about helping those who deeply desire to break through the daily challenges of loneliness, learn how to practice self-love, and who want to create intentional relationships.

Following a devastating divorce in 2017, LeAnn dove into a deeply personal journey of healing, realigning her life as a single mom, and a shift in her career path. She transformed her life through spiritual mentors, mindful meditations, and transformational bodywork, among other practices, and wanted to share her process with other women and men going through similar life transitions.

LeAnn's coaching programs offer guidance on how to shift your mindset around divorce, dating, being a better parent, and creating balance around your co-parenting dynamic. She created the "Realigning with Purpose®" process focused on 3 key pillars: Clarity, Letting go, and Integration. These 3 pillars help people connect to themselves, appreciate what they have in their lives, and gain an understanding of what they want, how to ask for it, and set personal boundaries.

LeAnn is currently writing her first full-length book and is a contributing author. She can be found through speaking engagements, on multiple podcasts and platforms such as Aloha Life, Uncharted, Her Nation, Magical Moments with Alena Chapman, Everything From A to Z with Arianne Zucker, and The Forward Female.

LeAnn Lazar Coaching has been empowering individuals and clients since 2018, as they heal, realign their lives, and create meaningful connected relationships. LeAnn would love to help you too!

**Contact LeAnn:**

LinkedIn: https://www.linkedin.com/in/leann-lazar-96a3269/

Facebook: https://www.facebook.com/leann.lazar

Instagram: https://www.instagram.com/leannlazarcoaching/

Website: www.leannlazarcoaching.com

# Arriving Right on Time
## By LeAnn Lazar

If you had told me 5 years ago in the throes of a divorce I would have a thriving life coaching business and would be embracing another woman as a mother figure in my children's lives, I would have thought you were out of your mind! I had no idea that I would gain this type of relationship after an emotionally painful divorce but she has become an integral part of our lives. We jokingly call each other "sister wives" as we have a collective interest in the wellbeing of my children and support the family dynamic we have created. One of my biggest wins as a coach is the coaching I gave my ex -husband in his relationship with his girlfriend. She's coined as the "bonus mom". This is exactly why I started my coaching business. To help others create new ways of life for themselves after divorce or a major life transition.

My concept of working for yourself and entrepreneurship has been flowing through my veins since I was 15 years old. While others were focused on the "high school life" and deciding where they were going to college, I was working as a model in Tokyo and New York from ages 15 to 18 on breaks from school and every summer. At 17 I moved to London to fulfill a contract with Models One. This early life experience gave me the skills for managing myself, negotiating contracts, and understanding the value of using your strengths to create a non-traditional path and career. It gave me access to people and experiences that I otherwise would not have known. In the modeling, acting, or entertainment business you form very close connections with people you otherwise wouldn't know to create art, to create a project, to create something. There's a skill set that is highly developed when you're in that scenario multiple times especially from a young age. I was able to hone my skills in reading people, knowing when people were telling the truth or having integrity, connecting with new people and having a level of vulnerability with others that I didn't really know in order to create in a collaborative way.

From as early as I can remember I was always a go-to person to help others solve their problems, figure out the best options in a situation, and support others in their desire or vision for themselves. Eloquently coined the "life sorter" by friends and colleagues I knew my path was to help others create their best life. I've always been a motivator and a leader with regards to self-improvement, personal growth, and life goals. Truly fulfilled by helping others and giving insight into their questions or circumstances that they were looking to change. After working for about 5 years as a model I decided to take a break and go to college. For me this was a big decision to step out of a career for a period of time and invest in myself for my future in a different way. I got my psychology degree and began working in that industry for a while with a vision of becoming a psychologist and running my own practice. I'll admit it, my favorite TV sitcom growing up was "Growing Pains". LOL

My life took a different journey as I leaned into the opportunity to pursue a modeling career after college. I again was traveling the world, meeting new people, having different interactions and basically coaching people all over the world. I settled in New York in 2001 and decided to lay down some roots and make this my home. I then met my ex-husband who had a very parallel career path to mine and it worked well. We got married and I began to settle into a bit of a routine life with being a wife, having a full-time modeling career and being married to a Broadway actor. There was always the voice inside my head reminding me of my vision for having a therapy practice. I researched programs and would bring the ideas to the table for discussion with my husband for what I would be doing next especially when we had children. However, anytime I discussed my passion for being a therapist or any entrepreneurial ventures I was not supported by my husband. He liked who I was for him and the career that I had. I knew there was more inside of me and that I could have a larger impact in people's lives. I have recognized in my personal growth journey that my need for support and validation was because I lacked the confidence to truly step into my own passion for fear of it not working out or not being the "right" choice.

13 years into my marriage two kids later I was going through a divorce. It was devastating and life-changing and became the driving force for me to create a new life for myself and start my coaching business. I dove into a deep personal journey of healing, realigning my life as a single mom, and making a shift in my career path. I transformed my life through spiritual mentors, mindful meditations, transformational bodywork, among other  practices, and wanted to share my process with other women going through similar life transitions.  I gave myself permission to step into creating my coaching business and truly have had no regrets although have had multiple stumbling blocks along the way.

I knew that starting a business was going to be dicey, especially in the middle of so many changes happening in my life all at once. First I needed a steady flow of income to support myself and my kids. I was offered a virtual sales position with an aesthetic device start up company and I jumped right in. I had never worked in corporate America and was stepping into this space for the first time over 40! Holy cow! This company was a start up and so there was a lot of collaboration with leadership in driving sales and productivity within the company. This was the perfect place for me to develop my skills for how a business starts from the ground up and the inner workings of selling and ROI. I needed this job to help build my confidence as a business owner.

A few months later, I started my coaching business. It was bare bones with a focus on creating value for people and selling my services. The first year I did 10k. I was so proud of not only the money I was making but of the people I was helping. I then knew that in order for me to make this business sustainable for me I had to think about it differently and have a solid business plan, marketing budget, backend system…all the things. I didn't have the cash flow to invest in the areas I needed so I continued to lean into doing all the things myself which lead to  my inevitable overwhelm and burn out.

I began to doubt my ability to maintain the momentum I needed to keep going in my business. I was making consistent money with my company and had moved into higher positions very quickly. The juggle of wearing all the hats was taking its toll on me. I would shift my energy into my job and then into my coaching and then into mom mode. I was exhausted.

Then covid hit and as I saw my peers in the coaching community leaning in and marketing hard to maximize the need to help others during that time. I was focused on keeping my job and main form of income and managing my kids doing school from home between me and my ex. It was too much. So my coaching business was at a plateau and I didn't know, like many of at that time, what the landscape of life would be.

LA was locked down unlike anywhere else in the country during covid. My ex and I were both dating people, my relationship was winding down and his was on and off. My ex began asking me questions about his dating life and ultimately I started coaching him on his relationship. My ability to hold space for him and coach him in an unbiased manner had been one of my biggest achievements as a coach.

After months of coaching, my ex was able to move through some emotional obstacles and step into really putting himself out there for this relationship. Within that year, they moved in together and are now engaged. She called me once they got back together and said how grateful she was for how supportive I was in his happiness and their relationship. She said if it wasn't for me, they wouldn't have gotten back together. She does not have children and I gave her the opportunity to experience being a mom, which is something she always wanted. This is when our relationship started to unfold as two women allowing each other to be part of this new dynamic where there was room for everyone to feel loved, appreciated and one I had hoped we would have as we raise our children and live across the country from our families.

Together, we have created a healthy family unit where we are connected with one another and in appreciation of everything in our lives. My kids have a "bonus mom" and I have gained a deep friend almost like a sister wife, someone who is invested in my children, loves them and supports the dynamic I have with my ex.

As a coach I meet each client where they are and guide them to what result they are looking to create in their lives. My coaching programs offer guidance on how to shift your mindset around divorce, dating, being a better parent, and creating balance around your co-parenting dynamic. I created the "Realigning with Purpose®" process focused on 3 key pillars: Clarity, Letting go, and Integration. These 3 pillars help people connect to themselves, appreciate what they have in their lives and gain an understanding of what they want, how to ask for it, and set personal boundaries.

I am currently writing my first full length book and preparing for a few course launches around Dating and Co-parenting. I can be found through speaking engagements, on multiple podcasts and platforms such as Aloha Life, Uncharted, Her Nation, Magical Moments with Alena Chapman, Everything From A to Z with Arianne Zucker, and The Forward Female.

LeAnn Lazar Coaching has been empowering individuals and clients since 2018, as they heal, realign their lives, and create meaningful connected relationships. I would love to help you too! Stay Connected or shift your life...head to my website to download my FREE workbook *Realigning with Purpose®* or subscribe to my newsletter, follow me on social media, reach out for a free connection call!

Website: leannlazarcoaching.com

Email: leannlazarcoaching@gmail.com

LinkedIn: @LeAnnLazar

Instagram: @leannlazarcoaching

Facebook: LeAnn Lazar

Youtube: LeAnn Lazar Coaching

# Not Your Average Passive

## By Sarah Miller

eet Sarah, a successful entrepreneur who has stormed her way through various fields over the past decade. Since joining the mortgage servicing industry in 2012, Sarah's hard work and dedication have resulted in her climbing the ranks and become a well-respected figure in the industry. Alongside her successful career, Sarah has also ventured into the world of modeling, gracing the runway with her incredible poise and charm. However, her true passion lies in writing, and she has become an international bestselling author with her first anthology, Shattering the Stigma of Single Motherhood. Beyond her writing, Sarah is also a savvy investor and has created multiple passive income streams, allowing her to pursue her passions and spend time with her beloved family and dogs. When she's not busy reading or writing, you'll likely find Sarah sipping on her favorite cup of coffee, fully embracing the freedom and flexibility that comes with her entrepreneurial lifestyle.

**Contact Sarah:**

LinkedIn: https://www.linkedin.com/mwlite/in/hisarahmiller

Facebook: https://www.facebook.com/HiSarahMiller

Instagram: @hisarahmiller

Website: SarahMillerCo.com

# *Not Your Average Passive*
# *By Sarah Miller*

What if I told you you could keep your day job and generate a passive income you don't have to trade your precious time for? Times are changing, and we no longer need to rely on time for money transactions. I always knew that I wanted to start a business. I spent a lot of time stressing about it. "The Perfect Business." Does it even exist? What can I bring into this world that will leave an enduring impression on those I love and those I haven't met yet? I've studied my journal entries from the last 20 years and found a consistent theme. Me questioning why we are here.

What's our purpose while on Earth? What mission should I be on, and what's the end goal? Instead of thinking of existential crisis, think more of how we can make the most of our time. More of what's the recipe for internal fulfillment, happiness, and less stress and depression. In my two decades of journal entries, I found pages stained with tears from different experiences, happy stories, 'I can't believe that happened' stories, stories of love, heartbreak, the joys, ups, and downs of motherhood. Living life and being deep in the journey. Dreams of what kind of life I wanted to give to the family that I created, my wishes for my children to trust me, and knowing that I'm always on their team. They know they are always wanted and loved; no one will ever be above them. The security of having a solid parent that my dad gave me, I want to give to them. So, how does this tie in with starting a business? It does! Well, the outcome does.

My ultimate goal is to be free to do what I want with my time. Freedom means that if my son and I want to vacation on a whim next weekend, we can. If something happened to my corporate job abruptly, I wouldn't have to stress about paying the bills—more time to do good in the world and to help others. Often we place value on money or things, but one of life's most precious commodities is time. You can always make more money; you cannot make more time. Time is something that we cannot get back. Throughout my career, I've worked two and three jobs at once and have put in 80-plus hours a week at one job resulting in burnout; I don't shy away from hard work, and I love it, but being the sole provider for my family in a one-parent household, my child needs my time too. I earn a decent salary in my career, but it won't put me in the seven-figure club. Something that I started a while ago is brainstorming business ideas every morning after my morning run and during my first cup of espresso (the way to my heart is a double shot of espresso). Doing this allowed me to tune into my inner self, my inner hustler, if you will, unlocking a habit that turned money-making into a game. I realized I didn't need one "really good business" to get to where I wanted and didn't need to stress about what that would be. I needed multiple passive income streams that would bring in income while sleeping, at my desk solving bankers' problems, and at dinner with my family—generating money but not having to trade my time for it. I've watched inspiring individuals talk about this for years and finally understood what they were talking about. The goal is freedom of time and not trading your time for survival.

The more streams of income that I have, the safer I feel. For many years I was just like many in society, where I lived and survived off one source of income. Over the last decade, I've traded over 26,000 hours of my time for a little over a million dollars. I started there as an entry-level agent and worked my way up to leadership, being challenged daily, visually seeing a direct result of my work that consumers use. I love that part of my life, and I do love my career. In 2017, I witnessed the harsh reality of the corporate world: layoffs. My first experience seeing this was gut-wrenching; there have been more since then. At my level of leadership, there isn't much, if any, forewarning. No one knows until about 30 minutes until it happens, and you don't know if you're impacted until it's announced to the department. If you're in leadership, you won't know if you're impacted as a manager or if your team is on the list until it's go-time. It's scary, but it puts into perspective how much you need to control your income and how giving a company that power over you is a gamble– not a way I want to live.

Think about it, having one source of income and that source having the power to say, "We are coming upon hard times and can't afford to have you on board anymore. Unfortunately, we no longer need your services." Then just like that, that paycheck you have relied on for the last however long is suddenly gone.

Sure, there may be a severance package, but depending on who you are and your seniority at the company, you may need more than that to get by. Financial struggles after a layoff have been the reality for so many. It's dicey. I'm grateful and fortunate that I haven't had to experience a layoff personally. Still, I've experienced seeing my team and co-workers being laid off and dealing with the stress of finding another job to keep up with their lifestyle. It's a tradeoff. You must make yourself the best at your company, ensure that you're an asset and that they can't eliminate you no matter how bad the numbers are. Being that asset usually comes with putting in 50, 60, or 80 hours per week. I've been there and done that. It only gave me immense stress, panic attacks, my body shutting down, spazzing on cortisol, and putting on 100 pounds. Was it worth it in the long run? Sure, I love my job, but at what cost to be the best? Now I'm fighting to regain my physical and mental health.

When I started focusing on building something outside of my career, I didn't know what I wanted to do, what I could give to the world, or what I could create. I did, however, know that I wished for financial security, an asset to build generational wealth, freedom to enjoy life, and to enjoy and attain a level of success of being genuinely happy while appreciating the obstacles.

I grew up in a single-parent household with my entrepreneurial father. I watched him create successful businesses throughout my life. I get my work ethic and appreciation for the hustle from him. In my teenage years, he and I bred AKC (American Kennel Club) show dogs. We developed a love for the breed, Soft Coated Wheaten Terriers, throughout the years, and I remember him saying it was nice having the extra cash. It wasn't a mill; it was genuine, and we put a lot of effort into the health and socialization of the breed. He and I did it together; looking back, it was a highlight of my childhood. When my son was six, he wanted a pet. We were teetering on what breed, what kind of pet, all the questions. Then the lightbulb switched on. Soft-Coated Wheaten Terriers! I was already familiar with the breed; they were perfect family members. They don't shed, are medium-sized, are happy, playful, and great with children. I got on the AKC website and started researching reputable breeders.

We found a perfect match about 4 hours from where we lived. The breeders prioritized the health of the pups, and you could tell that they were in the business because they loved the animals, not for the money. Our first guy, Maximiliano, was born on May 15, 2017. We picked him up when he turned eight weeks old and have loved him ever since. Over the next few years, I leaned towards giving my son the same experience I had growing up, sharing a "business" with him, and teaching him how to navigate the profit and costs of operating a successful and ethical breeding business. A couple of years after bringing Max into our home, I returned to the AKC website, found another reputable breeder, confirmed bloodlines for mating, and found our girl, Isabella. Isabella Luna is the spark and the fire. If I had a daughter, she would probably have Isabella's demeanor. Within our AKC business, my son shows the dogs at American Kennel Club events. We limit the amount of breeding to keep offspring rare, as they are both champion bloodlines. The sire is studded a maximum of once yearly, and our dam will have five litters over her lifetime. Putting a maximum limit on her litter will keep her healthy and not stressed. Remember, we are keeping this ethical and not turning our furry babies into "cash machines." We take pride in the health of our animals and ensure we are creating healthy generations to share with others who love this breed.

This business model is more than a side hustle. It's a 15–18-year commitment with your furry family members. If you're not going to commit to them, this isn't for you. You must be committed to your animals, stay ethical, and ensure that the breed's integrity and health are at the forefront of your business. If your heart is only in it for the money, please do not pursue this. Statistically, 3.3 million dogs enter shelters annually, and over 500,000 are euthanized. Around 25 to 30 percent of dogs in shelters are purebreds. Because of this tragic statistic, we prioritize properly vetting everyone we do business with, both consumers and fellow breeders. Each of our animals gets microchipped. If one of our dogs ends up in a shelter, we will be notified and go to the shelter ourselves to retrieve the animal. We haven't had to endure that yet, and I wish that would never happen, but we have controls in place should it occur. My goal is to share the wonderful breed with other families around the country, educate, promote ethics, and create lasting memories with my child.

That business makes my heart happy and brings in a little extra money each year. It's more of a seasonal payout, though. I wanted to add an asset that would bring in a steady amount of cash each month that also required a low time commitment. It sounds like a far stretch, right? It's closer than you think. I found a mentor who had started an Automated Teller Machine (ATM) business. I was skeptical at first and observed from afar. However, the more I watched, the more intrigued I was. The concept is simple: buy machines, sort and tidy legalities, fund vault, receive transaction fees, recycle, and repeat. Hiring a mentor who has already been through this was a smart move. Sure, you could always do your research and figure it out yourself, but some wise advice I received years ago was to learn from people's mistakes and what worked for them. In some ventures, I stick to staying independent and navigating my lane, but some others, I find mentors who are where I want to be and connect with them. You can apply your own spin on the basics when you get down the basics.

After researching, researching, and researching, I invested and bought my first few ATMs. It was a leap of faith, and it was for the best. It's been wonderful and everything I expected it to be so far. Each ATM is in a high-traffic area and averages 300 transactions per month. This business model is a no-brainer for me and generates passive income 24 hours a day, seven days a week. I'm making my money work and earning money I don't have to trade my time for. Through mentorship, I learned how to negotiate contracts with businesses, navigate the legalities, and what to expect from a financial aspect. As with any business, there's an upfront cost. Downstream, it pays for itself within 6-9 months.

I didn't have a hefty cash reserve when I started this. I still work at my corporate job today and let the money that I make there fund my business startup costs. Staying frugal and living below my means, for the most part, was imperative to me being able to start these. Don't get me wrong, I love to shop as much as the next person and sometimes indulge. I figured out that I needed to make my money work for me to get to where I wanted to be. Also, I don't need to spend all my money trying to give off the appearance of having it all together. I need to stick to my plan to have it all together. Taking care of the debt that I accumulated in my 20s to get my credit score in excellent standing also benefited me in more ways than one. I encourage taking care of that; it will make your life easier.

In addition to ethical breeding and ATMs, I also have a Short-Term Rental Arbitrage business. If you haven't heard of this business model, it's pretty interesting. It focuses on leveraging other people's properties through sublease agreements and renting them on platforms like Airbnb, VRBO, etc. Essentially, you rent properties long-term from the owner, and with appropriate contracts and agreements, you sublease those properties as short-term rentals and can charge a more significant rate than what you pay for the long-term rental. I also have other businesses, but to keep your attention in this chapter and conclude my piece, I will leave you with those three.

I did not have much money in the beginning to apply my ideas. I've been a single mother since I was 19 and have continuously operated in a single-income household. I completed three semesters of university and didn't have a degree to fall back on. I started my career at the entry level and worked my way up. I'm the product of hard work, love, and determination not to be another statistic. I will be the first millionaire in my family; I will ensure my children's children are set up financially and will have the knowledge to leverage and harness their power. I used to focus on getting approval from others. It's something that I struggled with for years from certain people in my life. I don't care about that anymore.

My child is proud of me, and that's enough. Everything else is just extra. As I said in the beginning, growing up, I knew I always wanted to start a business, but I stressed more about what kind of business and how it would play out. As time passed and I started researching and making small strides, things happened organically and weren't that stressful. Everything fell into place. I make every effort to approach my life with gratitude. It took many years of self-reflection to know who I am and to love who I am. To understand that I like what I do and how I do it. I realize that I love and appreciate the mistakes I've made, and I like the way and pace at which I learn from my mistakes and others. I don't want to be anyone else but me. Knowing this, I want to continue figuring out who I am and perfecting my frequency.

Creating side businesses has become a consistent activity. When you get the basics down, it flows freely. By staying consistent with my approach and reinvesting the surplus from my salary into cash-flowing assets, I've generated thousands extra each month that didn't require me to trade my time. Want to join me? Check out my contact information below. Thanks for reading this chapter.

I look forward to connecting with you in the future!

Here's a quick recap of transitioning to this lifestyle:

1. Get a routine down. Get enough sleep, schedule focused work hours, and ensure you care for your mental and physical health. That means getting some sort of exercise routine down and sticking to it. It doesn't need to be tedious, but sticking to a routine promotes discipline when you go on days that you don't feel like it. That discipline will flow into other aspects of your life. It will also keep your mental health balanced. Eat whole foods, and stay away from processed junk. All this impacts everything else.

2. Get your credit in order. Have consumer debt? Work on paying it down so you're prepared to take on a business investment when the opportunity presents itself.

3. Research side-hustle ideas daily. There are so many out there.

4. Keep reinvesting in your businesses and buy more cash-flowing assets with your profits.

5. Keep your 9-5 job. Don't quit when your assets start bringing in a little money.

@HiSarahMiller

Talk soon,

# True Success Comes From Genuine Passion and Drive

## By M.H. Ta, DDS

**D**r M.H. Ta was an Assistant Professor of Restorative Dentistry at LECOM and serves as a General Dentistry Preceptor at the LECOM School of Dental Medicine. Dr. Ta completed her undergraduate education at the University of Rochester in Rochester, N.Y., with the degree of Bachelor of Science in Microbiology. Upon completion of her undergraduate work, Dr. Ta matriculated at the State University of New York at Stony Brook, School of Dental Medicine, graduating with the degree of Doctor of Dental Surgery (DDS). Dr. Ta then spent a year at the University of California at San Francisco for her residency in Advanced Education in General

Dentistry. She has practiced dentistry since 1995, treating patients from all walks of life, in all phases of general dentistry, in Manhattan, New York, N.Y. Throughout her career, Dr. Ta has furthered her education at New York University, obtaining certificates in Advanced Continuing Education, Full-Mouth Reconstruction, Implantology: surgical and prosthetic treatment, and Advanced Aesthetics. Dr. Ta has also traveled on volunteer missions, such as Operation Smile and Cardio start, to help under-served dental needs populations overseas. She is married to a wonderful husband who is native to Florida. They have a handsome 12-year-old son and three adorable dogs. Dr. Ta enjoys cooking, swimming, collecting gems, traveling abroad for volunteer work, taking advanced dental courses, and spending time with her family.

**Contact M.H.:**

LinkedIn: https://www.linkedin.com/in/siesta-village-dentistry-53075b200/

Facebook: https://www.facebook.com/myhuong.ta

Facebook: https://www.facebook.com/siestadentist

Instagram: https://www.instagram.com/siestavillagedentistry/

Website: https://www.siestavillagedentistry.com/

# True Success Comes From Genuine Passion and Drive
## By M.H. Ta, DDS

The fireworks display on a lunar New Year's Eve started slow and steady with flowery swirls of red, blue, and gold sparkles, bright against the night sky. I watched as billions of tiny sparkling stars waterfall down towards the Earth. The noises became louder and overlapped with each other, accompanied by hundreds of colorful swirls of gold, red, blue, purple, white, and green sparkles. They filled and illuminated the sky with inlays of sparkly gemstones that seemed to float, disperse, and slowly disappear, replaced with many other colorful swirls in the round, elongated, starburst shapes in a fantastic magical light show for a good thirty minutes. The festive smell of firecrackers from the neighbors, the bustling footsteps, the loud cackling laughter and voices from my parents, sister, and brothers playing card games for real money, together with the succulent aroma of pork belly stew, banana leaves wrapped sticky rice with pork and beans, made all my senses complete with happiness and contentment.

"Ouch!" The sharp shooting pain had started again, contrasting with the epic euphoria of the New Year's Eve fireworks display I had witnessed. I suddenly realized the imminent toothache that I had ignored earlier that day. When I looked into the mirror, I noticed the left side of my face swelled up the size of a walnut. I had not complained or told my mom because I wanted to avoid the inevitable visit to the dentist. I eventually extracted the tooth myself, with a string tied to my room's doorknob, and then closed it forcefully to remove the wiggly tooth. It was not a good experience.

My Name is My-Huong Ta, also known as Nini. I was given both names at birth. The latter was supposed to be used by my family and relatives. My father was a South Vietnamese Army Major. The Southern military allied with the US military before 1975. At that historical time when the Vietnam war ended in 1975, The Northern communist (the VC) had taken over every aspect of life in South Vietnam.

Because of the ties with the US, our family had to move out of our home and go to the new economic zone in the mountains. My siblings and I could not attend college or obtain desirable jobs for this political reasons. The entire country was oppressed. Freedom of rights was taken away by the communist party. The right to live, travel, open businesses, and to higher education was controlled by the Party. In 1981, I made a political escape with my father and one of my brothers at age thirteen. We were called the boat people from South Vietnam in search of freedom. At sea for seven days and nights, a typhoon nearly took our lives together with 12 others. The brush of death came close that night when the storm lifted our boat vertically and broke a hole in the bottom of the wooden boat. We decided to sail back towards Vietnam for about 80km, to avoid further damage. We miraculously lived to tell the tale. Our adventure to escape was made more exciting with the accompaniment of schools of sharks and dolphins throughout the trip. The color of seawater turned purple to deep dark blue alternatively, in the South China sea's average depth of 3976 ft. We eventually sailed close to the Philippines island, Mindoro, and were rescued by one of their fishing boats. We watched our little tiny twenty feet wooden boat sink minutes after we got on board.

Due to my father's military history, we gained entry as political immigrants into the US. Of all the beautiful warm cities in the US, we got granted to assimilate into the American culture in the brutally cold, snowy lake-effect town of Rochester, New York. At the time, the cultural and language barrier shock of seeing teenagers kissing at lockers in high school, teenage pregnancies, my classmates talking back to our teachers without respect, and their laughs whenever I read in class. To make it more interesting, some of my classmates' occasional middle fingers told me to return to China. All of those unique events made me want to learn English and assimilate at a faster pace. I eventually became the Valedictorian of my class of 1986.

I went on to the University of Rochester and attained my BS degree in Microbiology while I was planning to prepare for the entrance exam into dental school. Oh yes, let me circle back to my dental condition. At this time, I had managed to get a cleaning after so many years of neglect. I was petrified of extraction, so I still had a few primary teeth fragments in my mouth. The future dentist in me decided to remove them successfully with some tweezers. I know, I know. Please do not attempt to do this after reading my short story.

In 1990, I received a full tuition scholarship for my dental school from New York State. I also gained acceptance to multiple dental schools, including Columbia University, the University of Pennsylvania, SUNY at Stony Brook, and New York University. I decided to go to SUNY at Stony Brook because it was one of the best in dentistry, and it only accepted 35 students instead of 100-200 at a time. The competition for SUNY school of dentistry was very fierce. But the real reason was that my boyfriend, at the time, got accepted into the same medical school. Please only laugh a little at the last sentence.

I conquered dental school and got my DDS, Doctor of Dental Surgery, in 1994. The light at the end of the tunnel finally arrived after four arduous, painful years of learning with the medical students didactically, doing lab work, plus seeing patients until the midnight candles melted daily. Residency in 1994-1995 became a piece of cake after the hell that the dental school put us dental students through. I then went to UCSF ( University of California at San Francisco) for a general dentistry residency. During my time in the bay area, I worked hard at hospitals during the day and enjoyed nightlife until the break of dawn, trying to make up for lost time as a former nerd.

For four years, I gave back to the needy by working in the inner city community dental clinic in Rochester, New York. Afterward, I worked in private offices until 2001 and started my first office in Manhattan, New York. I had very little savings, but with what I had borrowed from a generous friend, Maria, I had some additional cash to make a bold offer on an office for its equipment and location in midtown East of Manhattan, near the United Nations building. My office's grand opening was on September 13, 2001, just three days after the 911 incident.

I had no business experience, so I relied on my wits, instincts, and advice from mentors and friends for the business aspect. I placed ads, networked to meet people, made friends, signed on to insurance plans, made some TV commercials, and joined in with the communities in different charities. Word-of-mouth advertising helped my practice, in addition to the techniques mentioned above. The rent and office expenses in NYC were high compared to other cities, but with much care, effort, love, and passion for dentistry, I practiced dentistry in NYC for seventeen years. The rewards for my hard work were my first home in Long Beach, New York, a studio in Manhattan near my office to avoid the hectic daily commute, with the sometimes crazies on public transportation, and I paid back my loan. All this time, I never stopped learning and excelling in dentistry, as I gained more confidence in the business world. I took many advanced courses at NYU in Full Mouth Reconstruction, Advanced Aesthetic Dentistry, Implant placement and prosthetics, Botox, Bone grafting techniques, PRP techniques, etc. I sold my NYC practice, and many buyers/dentists were pleasantly surprised at my small practice's production/collection. It was just a three-workspace office of 850 sq ft.

After twenty-two years of clinical dentistry, I finally got exhausted and became jaded by the hustle and bustle of NYC's living. I applied for the Assistant Professor position at LECOM school of dental medicine in Bradenton, Florida, and accepted the role for two years. Teaching was rewarding, but the administration/corporate politics coupled with the slow pace the dental students were learning compared to a full-fledged dentist made me bored and missed clinical dentistry. I stopped teaching and traveled all over Asia for adventures and volunteer work for two months. Afterward, I set out to find a location to lease and start my second office in 2020.

During the pandemic, when locking down and staying six feet apart were the norm, sneezing and coughing were frowned upon, and endless debating on Covid-19 immunization shot safety and politics affecting our lives, I decided to start my second practice. I set out to acquire a space in our famous Siesta Key beach town. No dentist wanted to buy or lease, and many closed down. I negotiated the best possible lease and equipment location deals. I seized the opportunity for a good location, not knowing how the economy and the islanders would impact my future practice. I took a calculated chance. Bank of America and Chase were eager to give me the loan before the pandemic, yet they withdrew all loans at that time. Only TD Bank talked to me and asked me to write up my plan and proposal. I spent countless hours writing my proposal and plan with a three-year prediction for my future office. Twenty-five years post dental graduate, I finally knew how to negotiate with lawyers, bankers, sellers, and landlords. I was the driving captain for my contracts to put out demands and made compromises with all those involved to secure my second practice on the beautiful Siesta Key.

I had only a few patients call for at least three months to make appointments. I spent my time walking around the island, passing out my cards and flyers, talking to merchants and residents, eating out at different restaurants daily, and putting out flyers through the post office to all residents. I even got some write-ups for my practice via the Siesta Sand. The reporter wrote a lovely autobiography about my education. I threw an office holiday party and a grand opening party. The important thing was to be visible at all times positively. I joined charities and made a difference by helping the needy in the Sarasota and Bradenton communities.

Throughout it all, I have remained involved with Operation Smile since 2005. Through their organization, I went on a few missions overseas. I am the only American dentist in the Operation Smile team selected for the Cairo, Egypt mission to treat 400 children and give a presentation to exchange knowledge with local Egypt and other international dentists. I also belonged to CardioStart, a charitable heart surgery team. When we went overseas to treat and teach, I was the only dentist to ensure no dental infection before heart surgeries. As I write this chapter, I am also preparing a lecture about children with cleft lips and palates for Operation Smile Egypt March 14-18, 2023.

After two and a half years at my second practice in Siesta Key, a start-up dental practice with zero patients, I now see patients daily. Some come from different cities, states, and many local residents. They have supported my practice and searched me out for what I am so passionate about for the last twenty-f years. I have met up with all the predictions for my proposal with TD Bank, and I could pay back my loan at any time if I wish at the present moment. My education includes full mouth reconstruction, aesthetic dentistry, implant, and general dentistry. My dental passion, love, and compassion for people transcend all walks of life, occupations, ethnicities, races, sexes, medical conditions, religions, and politics. I only see people as genuine people who need my dentistry expertise. Using my skills to help people in need is my true success!

I miss the fireworks display and aromas of Vietnam's Lunar New Year festivities. Whenever I return to Vietnam, I accompany my visits with a volunteer mission to change lives. I no longer suffer toothaches during New Year's Eve celebrations, thanks to my dental work. I aim to educate children and adults on dental hygiene and oral health issues so no one should spend a holiday in pain.

My contact, website, and social media links are below:

https://www.siestavillagedentistry.com/

Follow me on Facebook:

https://www.facebook.com/siestadentist?mibextid=LQQJ4d

Follow me on Instagram:

https://instagram.com/siestavillagedentistry?igshid=NzAzN-2Q1NTE=

# Rising from the Ashes: Creating a New Life After Burnout

## By Dr. Kristen C. Eccleston
## The NeuroDiverse Teacher ™

D r. Kristen C. Eccleston (The NeuroDiverse Teacher™) is an award-winning education consultant, keynote speaker, published author, and mental health thought leader. Her areas of focus as an education consultant are K-12 and Corporate mental health and neurodiversity engagement. As an education consultant, she has worked with thousands of students and families in addition to some of the major global management consulting firms.

Dr. Eccleston's education history includes a Doctor of Education in Mind, Brain, & Teaching from Johns Hopkins University, a Master of Science in Special Education from Johns Hopkins University, and a Certificate in Educational Leadership and Administration from Hood College. She is an Adjunct Professor at Towson University in their Secondary and Special Education Graduate Programs. Additionally, she is a previous National Board-Certified Teacher: Exceptional Needs Specialist and holds an Advanced Professional Educator Certificate.

**Contact Kristen:**

LinkedIn: https://www.linkedin.com/in/kristen-eccleston-the-neurodiverse-teacher-keynote-speaker/

Facebook: https://www.facebook.com/The.NeuroDiverse.Teacher

Instagram: https://www.instagram.com/the.neurodiverse.teacher/

Website: https://www.theneurodiverseteacher.com/

# Rising from the Ashes: Creating a New Life After Burnout
## By Dr. Kristen C. Eccleston
## The NeuroDiverse Teacher ™

> *"Rock bottom became the foundation on which I rebuilt my life."*
> *- J.K. Rowling*

Rock bottom can be a terrifying thing, especially when less than a year prior, you felt like you were on top of the world. However, just like the quote from the famous Harry Potter author J.K. Rowling says, rock bottom can also be a catalyst that leads to the creation of a new and exciting life that you never thought possible. In this chapter, I want to share a story about life after burnout. Burnout can leave you feeling lost, hopeless, and unsure where to turn next. But, with the right tools and mindset, you too can build an extraordinary life you never imagined possible.

Growing up, I was what teachers would call a social butterfly, pleasant to have in class but unable to get their head out of the clouds and focus on the task. Teachers and loved ones frequently would remind me how smart I was, but I just needed to try harder. Unfortunately, I didn't learn until I was 30 that I am a neurodiverse individual with inattentive ADHD.

Having experienced being a student with undiagnosed ADHD, I understand firsthand the challenges of navigating school and feeling like you don't quite fit in. However, it was also through this experience that I discovered my passion for helping students who may be struggling in similar ways. After having what I can only describe as a tumultuous high school career, I entered college having no idea what I wanted to study or ultimately apply myself to professionally—other than being on Broadway, but that's a different story for another day. Eventually, I settled on becoming a communications major. In high school, I interned at a local radio station and figured that building on that experience made the most sense. By the time I graduated from college, I had switched my communications focus from mass media to public relations and was determined to slay at a corporate level. However, it didn't take long after my first job in public relations to realize that a career involving my sitting at a desk for most of the day was not for me. Then one day, as if the fates aligned, I had a chance encounter with a family friend that was an administrator at a local high school. During our meeting, the two of us talked in-depth about teaching, and it was at that moment I realized how excited I was over the thought of becoming a special education teacher.

As if this decision was preordained, there just happened to be a partnership program currently taking applications for individuals looking to earn a master's in special education between the school district I graduated from and Johns Hopkins University. What was even better, the school district would pay for your master's in return for three years of teaching service. What started as a new direction forward in my life turned out to be the most challenging and unique professional experience that I will forever be grateful to the universe for providing me. Don't get me wrong, teaching is by no means without its challenges, heartbreaks, and tears, but working with students has been one of the most rewarding adventures. Ultimately, becoming an educator helped me find my purpose. Not only did I get to feel empowered by helping students to find their strengths and abilities. I also discovered my true identity as a learner and uncovered skills and abilities I never knew I had.

Within a decade of my teaching career, I had many achievements. I became a National Board Certified Teacher, earned a certificate in Education and Leadership from Hood College, and created a new special education program for my district. As someone who loathed school as a student, to say I was proud of these accomplishments would be an understatement.

Having the opportunity to create a new special education program was one of the highlights of my professional career. It ultimately motivated me to earn a Johns Hopkins University doctorate in Mind, Brain, and Teaching. The program was designed specifically for high school students coping with mental health challenges that included but were not limited to concerns with suicidal ideation, self-harm, and school avoidance. The program's first several years were challenging, but I was riding an incredible high by year four. The program and I were honored by our district's Parent Teacher Association as Outstanding Special Education Program of the Year, and I was named a Special Educator of The Year. The year prior, the Board of Education honored me with the title of Distinguished Service to Public Education. Despite being in its early stages of development and growth, the program surpassed all my expectations. Witnessing the program's positive impact on students who were previously struggling with school avoidance and mental health issues, and seeing them thrive, graduate, and pursue promising futures, was beyond anything I could have hoped.

As I prepared to enter the fifth school year of the program, I felt like I was on top of the world, but nothing could have prepared me for what would come next. In just one year, my life began spiraling out of control in a way I never thought possible. I was in my third year of a doctoral program and stressed beyond belief, but the stress of being back in school was nothing compared to what was about to come my way. I still vividly remember the day I received a phone call informing me that one of the teachers I supervised was having an affair with one of our students. Although I had no idea about the relationship between the two and couldn't think of one red flag that would have indicated a cause for concern, I still felt like I had somehow failed one of my students. There are no words to describe the feelings of despair that I cycled through and the heartbreak I faced as a result. Then, adding to the stress, I learned that another one of my students had experienced a psychotic break and was threatening harm to all of my staff on social media and, unfortunately, had access to weapons. For weeks I jumped from meeting to meeting, trying to get a handle on both of these devastating situations.

Then, as I was driving home from work one day, my doctor called to inform me that I needed surgery to remove a large kidney stone that had formed. Soon after, my mom was diagnosed with throat cancer. And, if things were not heavy enough, I suffered an ankle injury after falling down a flight of stairs. My fall led to six months in a medical boot. It seemed as though everything that could go wrong did, and the cumulative effect of these events left me feeling hopeless and shattered.

Unfortunately, I didn't realize I was burning out until it was too late. Looking back, even before all of the events that led to my breakdown, there were signs that something was off - I was constantly tired, irritable, and had a hard time focusing on tasks that used to come easily to me. But I brushed it off as everyday stress, thinking things would improve if I pushed through. It wasn't until my world came crumbling down that I realized how deep my burnout was. I was emotionally drained, physically exhausted, and I couldn't seem to find any joy in the things that used to make me happy. It was a painful realization that I had ignored the signs of burnout for so long, and now I was paying the price. It was a wake-up call to take my mental health more seriously and to prioritize self-care moving forward.

Ultimately, by prioritizing my self-care, I had to make one of the hardest decisions of my life: leaving behind my career as a special educator and a program I had built from the ground up. For years, I had poured my heart and soul into the program, and it had become a significant part of my identity. However, I realized that the long hours, high-stress situations, and constant demands overwhelmed me in a way that had far surpassed simply being burnt out. If I wanted to be available as a mother and a wife, something had to give. Choosing my mental health over my career was one of the hardest things I had ever done, but deep down, I knew it was the right decision. However, even though I knew I had made the right decision, almost immediately, I began to struggle with feelings of guilt, shame, and disappointment in myself for leaving a profession that had always meant so much to me.

With time, I realized that my mental health was more important than any job, and I needed to prioritize taking care of myself. However, deciding to leave was just the beginning. I felt trapped in my mental health hell for two and a half years. Every day was a constant battle with anxiety and depression. I felt lost and unsure about the future, afraid of some new and unexpected tragedy at any moment. It was difficult to see a way out of the darkness and to imagine a future where I felt happy and fulfilled. I felt like I was constantly fearing, worrying about what would happen next, and feeling like I had no control over my life. It was a painful and isolating experience, and I often felt nobody understood what I was going through. But with the help of therapy, support from loved ones, and a lot of hard work, I slowly made progress toward a brighter future.

Grieving the old version of myself was a difficult but necessary part of my journey toward acceptance after burnout. It was hard to let go of the person I used to be - the one who could handle a heavy workload without breaking a sweat, was always up for a challenge, and felt like she had it all together. But the truth was, that version of myself wasn't sustainable, and it had led me to a place of burnout and exhaustion. Accepting the new version of myself felt like a daunting task at first. Still, as I started to focus on self-care and healing, I realized there were many positive qualities in the new version of myself I had developed during my journey. I was more compassionate, patient, and understanding of my limitations. I learned to set boundaries and prioritize my needs rather than constantly putting others first. Though it was a painful process, accepting the new version of myself was a necessary step towards healing and finding joy again.

After experiencing burnout, finding myself again felt like a miracle. For so long, I had felt like a shell of my former self, going through the motions without real purpose or joy. But as I started to prioritize self-care and take steps towards healing, I slowly began to feel like myself again. I reconnected with hobbies and activities I had abandoned, rediscovered my passions and interests, and started feeling more present and engaged in my relationships with others. Though the journey toward rediscovering myself was difficult, the rewards were immeasurable, and I felt grateful for the opportunity to start anew. The joy of finding myself again was indescribable, like a weight lifted off my shoulders. It was a reminder that even in the darkest times, there is always the potential for healing and growth.

With my renewed sense of purpose, I found a new career in education consulting, which was a dream come true. After going through my struggles with burnout and mental health, I knew that I wanted to use my experiences to make a positive impact on the lives of others. In this role, I can work with families of students struggling with mental health needs and provide them with the tools and resources they need to thrive academically and social-emotionally. I assist parents every step of the way by participating in school meetings and helping to locate resources and supports that will empower their child to reach their full potential. Additionally, I have used my experience with burnout to find my voice in a way that allows me to share my message of struggle and triumph with others who have faced similar hardships. By speaking openly about my experiences, I hope to inspire others to prioritize their mental health journey and recognize that they are not alone in their struggles.

Looking back, I'm amazed at how far I've come since experiencing burnout. Leaving behind my old career was difficult, but it was ultimately the right choice for me. It allowed me to prioritize my mental health and make room for new opportunities I would never have experienced if I had stayed stuck in my old ways. Such as becoming the second runner-up on The Blox, "the largest competition tv show on the planet," being selected to be a TEDx Speaker, or receiving an award in Las Vegas for Outstanding Leadership in Education. Now, I'm excited to wake up each day and know that I'm making a positive impact on the lives of others in my career as an education consultant and speaker. And as I move forward, I hope to have future opportunities to share my story with others who may be struggling with burnout or mental health challenges. If my journey can provide just a bit of inspiration or hope to others, it will have been worth it. The future is full of exciting possibilities, and I'm grateful to be moving forward with a renewed sense of purpose and passion.

If you want to learn more about me or my work as an education consultant or keynote speaker, please visit my website at www.the-neurodiverseteacher.com. You can also follow me on social media @ the.neurodiverse.teacher (Instagram & TikTok).

I look forward to connecting with you!

# Getting Out of My Own Way

## By Adrienne Kennie

Adrienne Kennie was born and raised in Austin, Texas where she currently resides. She received a Bachelor of Science degree in Health Administration from Texas State University and a Master's degree in Business Administration from Concordia University. She also completed the Women's Entrepreneurship program with the Bank of America Institute at Cornell University. She is currently a Management Consultant for a large consulting firm. During her free time, she enjoys spending time with family and friends, making arts and crafts, traveling, writing, and most of all her role as mom to her one-year-old daughter. Adrienne is the CEO and Founder of 28th State Business Solutions, LLC, and is currently working on other projects to promote her passion and goals to help others. Adrienne is also a co-author of Shattering the Stigma of Single Motherhood.

**Contact Adrienne:**

LinkedIn: https://www.linkedin.com/in/adrienne-kennie-80ab3327

Facebook: https://www.facebook.com/adrienne.kennie

Instagram: https://instagram.com/msnikki_81?igshid=ZDdkNTZ-iNTM=

Website: https://www.28thstatebusiness.com

# Getting Out of My Own Way
## By Adrienne Kennie

## How It All Began

As a young child, I had an awareness of success and achievement and always aspired to be successful in my education and everything that I did. My vision of success was achieving the American dream by having a professional career with an amazing title, making six figures, owning a nice home, having a large bank account, and having three kids, I simply just wanted it all. I grew up in a household where we had everything we needed, although we didn't always have everything we wanted. We did have struggles at times, but we made it through.

Both of my parents dropped out of high school and obtained their GEDs later in life, so they wanted better for my brothers and me. I remember being in elementary school believing that I needed to do well in school to achieve the American dream goals that I had set for myself. I was in honors classes, won scholarships, and I was one of the top ten African American seniors in my graduating high school class. I felt as if I was on the right path to being successful.

When I started college, I knew that I wanted to major in the health field. I had been fascinated with the healthcare field since my part-time position at a local doctor's office in high school. I was responsible for checking patients in and out, verifying benefits, and assisting the chiropractor, physician's assistant, and physician. I didn't realize it then but that's when I began to learn the day-to-day operational processes in a medical practice. This was a skill that I was good at and enhanced as I got older. After grappling with the idea of majoring in Physical Therapy, Health Administration, or medical school, I decided to major in Health Administration.

While attending college, I worked at the YMCA and managed their Membership Services department at two locations. I supervised staff, managed to schedule, helped members with financial assistance needs, attended monthly leadership meetings, etc. at the age of 21. After a few years of doing this, I decided to start building my health career and landed a position in Revenue Cycle Management a large health system. I was tasked with working in the ER at a level 1 trauma center. This was an eye-opening experience because I worked with underserved members who were homeless, uninsured, and disabled. I was happy to be able to help these members by linking them to community resources to ensure they were getting the care that they needed beyond the ER. I went from being a team member to being a leader. When there was an opening on the business side, I became an office manager where I was able to lead teams and manage the day-to-day operations of a group of gastroenterologists and a group of general surgeons. I was beyond grateful for the opportunities that I had in my 20s.

These opportunities helped shape my career experience, and earning my bachelor's degree in Health Administration led to even more opportunities. I then went back to school and graduated with my Masters in Business Administration and decided to learn more about the health insurance industry. This paved the way for my journey as a Management Consultant for a large consulting firm.

## Upward Progression

When I started working as a Management Consultant, I finally felt as if I had gotten to the level of professional success that I was looking for. I was making the money that I wanted to make. I was traveling every week to help clients in various cities, and I had just purchased my first home. I was beyond thrilled because I always wanted to be able to own a home and I felt blessed to be able to do this. I needed a win because life had thrown so many curveballs my way. As a consultant, we worked with various clients and helped them solve business issues. I always joked that I should start my own business, but I got so wrapped up in work that I didn't pursue the opportunity. I was helping companies save millions of dollars, and I had even collected over a million dollars when I worked in revenue cycle management, I had the skillset and education to start my own business, but I continued to push the idea aside.

When COVID hit, everything changed. We went from traveling Monday – Thursday every week to being completely grounded and working remotely from home. Honestly, I was a bit relieved because the traveling was a lot. I wasn't traveling for personal gratification because I didn't have the time to do that. I was so consumed with work. I felt as if I was living out of a suitcase, and I wasn't able to enjoy my new home. I was also beginning to wonder if I was really living in my purpose and if this was where I needed to be professionally and personally. Professionally, I had the money and title but personally, I wasn't enjoying life to the fullest.

I did some research and decided to start a small business solutions company. I picked a name and submitted my LLC application. I also opened a business bank account. I was so proud of myself; however, work got in the way again and that is where my business attempt stopped. I got caught up with work and life and put the business on hold again. In February 2021, I found out that I was pregnant, and this was a life changer and saver for me.

## My New Reality

Becoming a mother was the greatest gift. I was on maternity leave and was solely focused on adjusting to motherhood and making sure my child and I were taken care of. I was extremely lucky to have 20 weeks off; however, when it was time to return to work, I was beyond nervous. We still weren't traveling, but I was afraid of what work combined with motherhood would look like. When I returned to work, I was hit with reality. My fears became real because I was in numerous meetings throughout the day, with no time to get actual work done. This meant working odd hours to get work done. I would set an alarm at 4 am just to get up and finish work and get things together for my daughter before she woke up for the day. I had absolutely no work-life balance. I had meetings at 7 a.m. when I had to get my daughter ready for daycare and had meetings after picking her up from daycare. It was a complete nightmare.

One day I had an evening meeting, and my daughter began hitting on my laptop keyboard. I was also having to speak on calls with my daughter crying in the background. That is when I realized that I needed to make a change. I couldn't continue doing this long term and did not feel that consulting provided the opportunity for me to have a work-life balance. Being a mom is the best role that I have ever had and I couldn't risk being a good mom for work. I was having more bad days than good and on Sundays, I was literally nauseous thinking about work the following day. I never realized the importance of having a work-life balance until I became a mother. I was struggling to meet all of the demands at work and felt that I was failing miserably and that I was weak. This was hard for me because I always felt that I needed to be strong and push forward no matter how hard things were. I felt that I needed to be a superwoman and accomplish it all. Being in the corporate world as a black woman I had to work harder, and I felt as if I could not afford to make mistakes. I needed to roll with the punches in order to be successful in corporate America at all costs. I had a heavy weight on my shoulders dealing with work challenges and being a single mother. This was a toxic working environment, and I knew that I had to do something fast because I felt as if my back was against the wall, and I had to make a choice between work and being a mother.

## Redefining My Purpose

I took some time off from work and spent time thinking about what I truly wanted to do with my life. I wrote a list of things that I wanted and realized that while I had spent years building my career, I completely let my personal needs and wants to suffer. One day I prayed and asked for guidance and clarity on what I should be doing, and I suddenly thought about medical billing services. Healthcare has always been my passion, I also love helping others, and love solving challenges. I had done a lot of work in healthcare and understood the billing processes, regulations, and coding, and with my years of consulting experience, decided to build a medical billing services business. I conducted research to understand requirements and began building a business plan. I also started buying study materials to prepare for the needed certifications. During this time, I realized that I spent years procrastinating and not living in my full purpose and truth. I always knew that I wanted to be a business owner, but rarely made time for myself. I put all of my time, and energy, into it and was practically killing myself to make money and meet goals for other companies. Now that I look back, it was fear that stopped me from starting my own business years ago.

## Putting Thoughts Into Action

Once I aligned on the medical billing business that I wanted to have, I was fully committed to making sure I would start making my dreams a reality. I created a project plan to hold myself accountable. I had to be honest with myself and realize that I was getting in my own way by having fears and doubts about starting my own business. In my self-awareness journey, I learned that there were so many things that I wish I had focused on sooner. I know that others may be struggling with self-sabotage and fears and my advice would be to implement the following steps to Get Out of Your Own Way:

1. Make the Time: Your dreams are important too

2. Invest In Yourself: If you don't invest in yourself, who else will?

3. Just Do It: Don't let fear or procrastination stop you from accomplishing your goals

4. Put One Foot in Front of the Other: Keep moving, Don't stop

5. Celebrate the wins: Every win, small or big is something to celebrate

6. Have No Regrets: Every opportunity is a learning lesson. Be grateful that you took the chance to try

7. Re-Assess: Where are you now? If everything is good, keep going. If there are opportunities, don't be afraid to pivot and try something new

I read these steps every day and have been motivated to keep going to achieve my dreams. I challenge others to do the same. I don't know what the future will hold, but I know that I will be happy not wondering what would have happened if I had made the effort to start. If you want to follow my journey or would like to reach out, I can be reached at:

Linkedin.com/in/Adrienne-kennie-80ab3327

https://www.instagram.com/msnikki_81

https://www.28thstatebusiness.com

# Writing Your Story: The Educator to Entrepreneur Journey

## By Meagan Beam

eagan Beam, the owner of OTTER Reading, passionately supports students and teachers in the foundational reading space. She has a bachelor's in special education from Clemson University, a master's in reading from Grand Canyon University, and 2 certifications in Orton Gillingham through Orton Academy. After 16 years, she has "retired" from the classroom and is now a curriculum specialist for Really Great Reading while simultaneously running her business.

She is a single mom to an amazing daughter, Madelyne, who also plays a major role in the business. She is the artist for all of the decodables! Madelyne is 15 years old and aspires to attend UNC-Chapel Hill to major in marine biology.

When Meagan is not working in the foundational reading space, she is spending time with Madelyne at UNC-Chapel Hill for women's soccer games, watching UNC basketball and Clemson football, or snuggling with her pups, Finley and Baxter (Aussie doodles).

**Contact Meagan:**

LinkedIn: https://www.linkedin.com/in/meagan-beam-454804266/

Facebook: https://www.facebook.com/otterreading

Instagram: https://www.instagram.com/otter_reading/

Website: www.otterreading.com

# Writing Your Story: The Educator to Entrepreneur Journey
## By Meagan Beam

Pencils. As educators, we have a love-hate relationship with them. We love seeing proof of light bulb moments, but they can be a PAIN! HA! We start the year with what feels like thousands of pencils and sink into this false hope this will be the first year we won't run out!

By January (if not before), reality sets in! We wonder where they all went and are sure they are part of our students' daily (nutritious?) diets. And don't get us started on the handheld pencil sharpeners students use 1 million times a day (no, seriously) or the thousands of times they get up to use the classroom pencil sharpener. These daily distractions lead to millions of thoughts lost by teachers and millions of dropped pencil shavings left over the floor.

But, as much as they drive us CRAZY (because, trust me, they do), pencils are proof of learning and growth happening in the classroom. New pencils are handed out all the time and offer a fresh start. Pencils get sharpened as students use them to learn and grow. Worn-down erasers show mistakes and growth are taking place. And just when the pencil seems too small to point (a student favorite) and is of no use, a teacher gives the student a brand-new pencil, a fresh start (but we know it's mainly to prevent it from being stuck in the pencil sharpener for the millionth time). Thus, the "life cycle" of the pencil starts all over again.

My entrepreneurial journey is similar to the pencil's "life cycle." There have been many fresh pencils, moments of sharpening, and multiple opportunities to erase mistakes. The most important thing

I could share is picking up the pencil, putting it down, and leave your mark! That's what I did, and I could never have imagined all the amazing opportunities that could have led to!

In June 2016, armed with a fresh pencil, I attended 80 hours of Orton Gillingham training. Joan Gerken (a Fellow through Orton Academy) led the movement, which changed my life as an educator. Orton Gillingham is a research-based, brain-friendly, systematic, prescriptive, sequential, and multi-sensory approach to teaching students how to read. This training led to two certifications in Orton Gillingham! The training I received became the foundation of my entrepreneurial journey.

I first picked up my pencil in October 2018. I was prepping to speak at a regional conference about teaching with a multi-sensory approach. At the same time, my students needed extra support for adding suffixes to words (especially the Y to I rule). I wanted my students to be able to take the y off physically, put on the I, and then the vowel suffix. I had never seen a tool that allowed students to do that (I looked!), so I decided to figure it out myself! I eagerly walked into a hardware store that evening, praying and searching for something to use. On the afternoon of October 29, 2018, I walked out of the hardware store armed with PVC pipes, couplings, a PVC pipe cutter, and the beginning of a story.

That night, I stayed up late cutting, writing on pipes and couplings, and prepping materials for my session. I wanted to be able to share my idea with the teachers too, but my hands barely survived the cutting! The following day, the room was full of teachers, and I was full of nerves. I loved sharing and collaborating with the teachers, and I hoped they could take ideas back to their classrooms to help increase student engagement and mastery! Collaboration was a vital pencil mark along my journey. But then I put my pencil down.

At this moment, my career as an educator began to change. My career looked like many small pencil dots (you know them, like the ones kids make in their erasers all the time!), and unbeknownst to me, they would all become connected! I realized the stress of teaching full-time in the classroom was too much on my body with my autoimmune diseases (Type 1 Diabetes and Fibromyalgia). I needed to figure out how I could give my body a break. But as a single mom, I still needed to earn a full-time income.

It was hard to admit this decision because I love teaching with every fiber of my being. I called my students my kids. I love them fiercely, and I advocate for them daily. I have a strong love and commitment to my students and their families, and I couldn't imagine erasing that out of my life! Leaving the kids, I cared so much about making the transition difficult to process, and man, was I sharpened throughout it. But I was excited about the fresh pencils and new possibilities ahead. I was even more excited to focus on reaching my goal of becoming a literacy specialist.

In the Fall of 2020, I made another pencil dot with a change to the tool! Instead of writing on it, I started cutting out letters. I even had teachers expressing interest in my device and wanting it for their classrooms. My first order was an entire photo box FULL of cut pipes and couplings, and it traveled from Charlotte, NC, to California! Manually cutting PVC pipes was a significant indention to my timeline (like the ones kids make on their desks with their pencils, UGH!) and started my entrepreneur journey. With the first few sales, I realized I better protect my tool! On April 30th, I filed my first provisional patent, which went pending!

A couple of months later, I had my tool listed on Etsy. My Etsy store started the journey of a lot of erasing! Interest in my device started picking up, and I needed to find a way to manufacture the tool quicker because I was cutting and cleaning it all by hand. This process took FOREVER, and I was constantly scouring for items to get this erased and crossed out for something else!! Unlike our students, I wanted to ERASE it and not cross out the mistake a million times! HA!

I tried using a saw, but I erased that quickly because it left rough edges, and I would probably lose a finger! I tried tossing them in the dishwasher to speed up the cleaning process. That was another erased mistake (did you know heat expands PVC!?)! Thankfully, a handheld electronic pipe-cutting machine was released, which sped up things tremendously! There were so many times I could have quit or given up. But I chose to persevere and gripped my pencil tight.

Then things started happening quickly, and it was a BLAST! It was like writing in cursive, and I didn't have time to pick up my pencil! I had so many different and exciting opportunities I could not believe I was able to be a part of! In the spring of 2021, I met with a company called Westminster Tech. They agreed to put my product on their website! I was so excited to have the validation of my tool from an established company!

I contacted a foundational reading curriculum company called Really Great Reading (RGR) that summer. They use a strategy called Heart Words in their curriculum, and I used it with my builders. I emailed them to share what I was working on. They responded quickly and asked if I wanted to become a contractor. I eagerly said yes! I could not believe I was finally in the literacy space. I was genuinely overjoyed and just so excited! I quickly grasped that pencil and got to work! One piece of advice I will share is: don't be afraid to reach out and ask! You never know what they will say! And who knows, they might just say YES! And it gets better! I now work for them full-time! I could not be more grateful to be a part of such a fantastic company (and the people are genuinely INCREDIBLE)!

In 2022, I was excited to build off the $7000 sales I had in 2021 and continue developing and enhancing my tool! I began to focus on marketing myself and my product through conferences! The first conference I attended was the NC Reading conference as an exhibitor. It was amazing and a HIT! The teachers loved it and kept coming to show others and ask me questions. I learned so much, and I had so much fun sharing it! I even had a couple of sales at the conference, which I couldn't believe! Even a phonological awareness curriculum company took a sample of my tool to share with teachers at their training! Soon after, I partnered with Kidzu Children's Museum in Chapel Hill, NC! Kids can play with my tool any time at the museum!

This validation gave me the confidence to start focusing on manufacturing. Man, was this manufacturing process a moment of growth and sharpening for me! Before production, the manufacturer gave me an image of the design and some technical terminology. An engineer designed the tool and 3D printed it as a prototype.

Suddenly my tool was no longer a round PVC pipe but a triangular prism, nameplate, type shape. I loved it and sent the STEP file to the injection mold company to have it manufactured. The manufacturer said the process would take over a month from start to finish. I asked about it, and they assured me it would not affect the form, fit, or function, so I approved it, but I should have asked for more clarification.

The samples I received had indentions right next to where the letters would be. I emailed them to ask about them. They apologized for not clarifying the explanations and told me they would make adjustments. However, after that, I was given an update for three weeks when I followed up. I found out there hadn't been any adjustments made to the design, AND they gave me an invoice for $750 to pay for the adjustments. I am generally not one to stand up for myself. But, I responded that I was uncomfortable paying the $750 for the adjustments. Thankfully, they agreed, and manufacturing began! This whole process which was only supposed to take a month, turned into a stressful 3-month ordeal (which I immediately protected with my second provisional patent).

I needed to complete the manufacturing process quickly because, at this same time, I got cast for an entrepreneur tv show called The Blox. The show would be the perfect opportunity to launch the new version of my tool! I was scrolling Facebook one morning and saw an ad about applying to be cast on an entrepreneur TV show called The Blox. It is a 24/7 live-in crash course on entrepreneurship! There were over 60,000 applicants, and I was selected! I couldn't believe it! I was ecstatic!

The week of filming Season 5 was an incredible experience! I could discuss my tool, collaborate, and connect with the most notable entrepreneurs! This chapter, the new podcast (Miss Educated), my ad in Times Square, and many other things directly resulted from the show! I cannot even begin to describe how powerful it was for me as an entrepreneur to learn and connect with others in the same space!

When I returned from The Blox, I immediately grabbed a new pencil, sharpened it, and went to work! Not long after, I got accepted into the Retail Lab program hosted by Flywheel! Flywheel provides a coworking environment that invites entrepreneurs to learn and collaborate! The Retail Lab is a 6-week program that ends with a pitch night. The top 5 pitch winners receive a $2500 grant! I was so honored to win and receive one of the grants! I immediately put it to good use! I used it to build a website to make my tool digital (made by one of the Blox judges)! It is incredible and FREE on my website!

I also learned so much from the Retail Lab; the collaboration, networking, growth, and opportunities were incredible! I pitched at 1 Million Cups and received helpful feedback on fine-tuning my packaging. I got accepted into the Venture Mentoring Service (VMS) through the Cabarrus Center. I have had 2 VMS meetings, which have been a game-changer for my business. I have amazing mentors leading and guiding me. I cannot even begin to describe my excitement and gratitude for their tremendous leadership! Their support and impact have just been incredible!

After the Retail Lab Program, I traveled to San Antonio as an exhibitor at the International Dyslexia Association (IDA) conference. It was so incredible. I almost lost my voice on the first day! The most impressive part of the conference was the partnership with Institute for Multi-Sensory Education (IMSE) I was able to form! It began when I was flying out to San Antonio over puppies! We realized that we both had puppies from the same breeder AND litter! We started talking "shop," and she told me she is the Director of Academics with IMSE. She is fantastic and SO supportive of my business!

After the conference, the IMSE Director asked if I would be interested in partnering with them! I was in shock! I could not believe that they wanted to partner with me! I replied YES! She told me IMSE wanted 20 K-2 bundles in inventory, and they would like their 100 trainers to have my tool to use when leading training! They train about 25,000 teachers a year! I could not believe it! And I need to get busy manufacturing the 8000 pieces!

My next stop was in Louisville, Kentucky, for the Council for Exceptional Children (CEC) Convention. This conference was just as unique! I could talk to many people about my tool, including American Printing House for the Blind and Lakeshore Learning! One of my favorite parts was talking to college professors at the conference! I loved hearing how they supported new teachers, and they were excited to take my information to share!

I've had a fantastic start to 2023, and it has only just begun! I am eagerly hovering my pencil above my paper to see what the future of OTTER Reading holds! I desperately want to make a difference in the literacy world and advocate for the millions of sweet children who are struggling readers. I have tools available on multiple platforms through my website at www.otterreading.com. There are even opportunities to grab a Give Back Bundle with an extra Letter A-Z set to gift to someone in need! Thank you for following along in my journey!

# Do YOU want to be an author, and have an inspiring story to share?

Dr. Jillian Zambon is always seeking inspirational stories to publish. Reach out to her today on Facebook at: https://www.facebook. com/jillian.zambon/

I can't wait to hear your story!